D0744240

THE BEETHOVEN VIOLIN SONATAS

The Beethoven Violin Sonatas

HISTORY, CRITICISM, PERFORMANCE

Edited by
Lewis Lockwood and Mark Kroll

University of Illinois Press
Urbana and Chicago

© 2004 by the Board of Trustees
of the University of Illinois
Maynard Solomon retains the copyright
to chapter 6
All rights reserved
Manufactured in the United States of America
C 5 4 3 2 1

⊗ This book is printed on acid-free paper.

Library of Congress Cataloging-in-Publication Data
The Beethoven violin sonatas : history, criticism, performance /
edited by Lewis Lockwood and Mark Kroll.
p.   cm.
Collection of essays "derived from a festival-conference on the
Beethoven violin sonatas held at Boston University in Oct. 2000,
directed by Mark Kroll and Lewis Lockwood."
Includes bibliographical references (p.) and index.
ISBN 0-252-02932-1 (cloth : alk. paper)
1. Beethoven, Ludwig van, 1770–1827. Sonatas, violin, piano.
2. Sonatas (Violin and piano)—Analysis, appreciation.
I. Lockwood, Lewis.
II. Kroll, Mark.
MT145.B422B4   2004
787.2'183'092—dc22   2003026966

MT
145
B422
B43
2004

Contents

Acknowledgments

The editors gratefully acknowledge the excellent work of Matthew Cron as editorial assistant for this book. Mr. Cron not only formatted all the music examples but also helped in many other ways in preparing this volume, including editing the texts, corresponding with authors, and communicating with the University of Illinois Press. We express our appreciation to the Consul General of Germany in Boston and the Boston University Humanities Foundation for their generous support of the Boston University International Beethoven Festival-Conference, at which the contents of this book were first presented. Our sincere thanks to the Beethoven-Haus Bonn, British Library, Deutsche Staatsbibliothek Berlin, Breitkopf und Härtel, and G. Henle Verlag for their help in granting permission to reproduce many of the musical examples and illustrations.

THE BEETHOVEN VIOLIN SONATAS

Introduction
Lewis Lockwood and Mark Kroll

Beethoven's sonatas for violin and piano have a central role in the history of keyboard chamber music. The first performances of these works aroused strong reactions from both audiences and critics, and their influence on later generations of performers and composers remains profound. Revered by nineteenth-century violinists and pianists, they remain classic works in the recital programs of modern performers. The recorded legacy includes many complete sets of the ten sonatas, as well as legendary recordings such as that of Opus 30, No. 3, by Fritz Kreisler and Sergei Rachmaninoff, and Opus 47 by Joseph Szigeti and Béla Bartók. As it developed after Beethoven, the genre included two important violin sonatas by Schumann, three by Brahms, and an important series of violin sonatas by French composers—Franck, Saint-Saëns, Fauré, and Debussy.

From his apprentice years onward, Beethoven had an intimate familiarity with the violin and its practitioners. Although he was trained primarily as a pianist and made his mark as a brilliant composer-pianist, he also had violin lessons at an early age. He occasionally played viola in the Bonn court orchestra, which included such superior violinists as Franz Ries and Andreas Romberg. When Beethoven moved permanently to Vienna in 1792, the Austrian capital's much larger musical scene afforded him contact with a far wider array of string players. These included the very young Ignaz Schuppanzigh, who was to remain a collaborator throughout Beethoven's lifetime, mainly as quartet leader but also as friend and all-purpose violinist. As early as 1798 Schuppanzigh played with Beethoven in the first performance of one of the early violin sonatas, probably one from the Opus 12 collection.

In the 1790s, as the young Beethoven was making his mark, a new generation of virtuoso violinists were making major strides in performance technique. Especially prominent were a group of French violinists who had been taught or influenced by the Italian master Giovanni Battista Viotti: Rodolphe Kreutzer, Pierre Baillot, and Pierre Rode. Beethoven met all three in Vienna between 1798 and 1810, and Kreutzer and Rode are closely associated with two of his best-known sonatas, Opus 47 (the "Kreutzer" Sonata) and Opus 96, Beethoven's last in the genre. The influence of Kreutzer, Baillot, and Rode was visible not only through their playing careers but in the jointly written *Méthode de violon* (1803), which became the standard violin treatise for the next thirty years.

In writing his violin sonatas Beethoven faced the challenge of blending his expanded styles of keyboard writing with a wider expressive range newly possible for stringed instruments. This genre enabled him to match his legendary ability to play legato with that of the violin. Accordingly, the violin sonatas are turning points in the history of the genre and of chamber music itself. They also offer an interesting perspective on Beethoven's compositional development.

Apart from Opus 96, the violin sonatas stem from 1798 to about 1803. Beethoven was then ending his first maturity and beginning his second, writing his first two symphonies, the *Prometheus* ballet, the first three piano concertos, the Opus 18 quartets, and the eleven piano sonatas that stretch from Opus 13 (the "Pathétique") to the three of Opus 31. In 1798, when he published his Opus 12 violin sonatas, he had not yet written his First Symphony; by 1812, the year of Opus 96, he was finishing his Eighth Symphony and was moving toward his last creative phase.

The received image of Beethoven has always stressed the epic qualities of the Third, Fifth, and Ninth Symphonies; the breadth of the "Razumovsky" Quartets; the expressive strength of the "Waldstein" and "Appassionata" Sonatas; and the deep philosophical content of the last piano sonatas and string quartets. Although this image is meaningful and enduring, it fails to make room for contrasting dimensions of Beethoven's art that belong to other aesthetic domains—those of grace, beauty, humor, and restraint, which emerge in the larger genres and in the more intimate world of his keyboard chamber music. Less studied and discussed than the string quartets, Beethoven's works for piano and stringed instruments—principally his violin sonatas, cello sonatas, and piano trios—form a vital group of works that deserve closer critical attention than they have yet received.

This book is a partial remedy for this neglect. To our knowledge it is the first collection of critical and scholarly essays devoted solely to the Beethoven violin sonatas. These essays, which deal with all ten sonatas, thus add to a very slim sheaf of published scholarly writing on this repertoire. They derive from a festival-conference on the Beethoven violin sonatas held at Boston University in October 2000 and directed by Mark Kroll and Lewis Lockwood.

Discussing Beethoven's earliest set, Sieghard Brandenburg presents an overview of the Opus 12 sonatas of 1798 as milestones on Beethoven's path to maturity. He focuses on Beethoven's indebtedness to his core models, the Mozart violin sonatas—above all Mozart's last works of this type, the E♭-major Sonata K. 380, and the A-major Sonata K. 526—and also on the character and reception of these first attempts in the genre. Two years later, in 1800, Beethoven composed the so-called "Spring" Sonata in F Major, Opus 24, a turning point toward a new and richer conception of the roles of the violin and piano. Lewis Lockwood's essay explores the special qualities of melodic beauty that have always been recognized in the opening themes of all three movements and the apparent importance of this aesthetic vein for Beethoven at this time. Opus 24 is also seen here in relation to its curious mate, the A-minor Violin Sonata, Opus 23, and to other Beethoven chamber works of this time. The three big sonatas of Opus 30 (1802–3) form the subject of Richard Kramer's chapter, which reflects on Opus 30 in the context of Beethoven's experimental aims as he moved toward a "new poetics" of the accompanied sonata. The monumental "Kreutzer" Sonata (1803) is then examined in essays by Suhnne Ahn and William Drabkin. Ahn discusses the qualities of balance and virtuosity in this brilliant sonata, about which Beethoven wrote that it was "written in a highly concertante style, almost that of a concerto." Drabkin centers attention on the work's tonal organization, beginning with the unusual harmonic plan of the slow introduction. He also develops interesting parallels with two later chamber works in the same key (A major) by Mendelssohn and Dvořák. The final stage of Beethoven's engagement with the genre is the G-major Violin Sonata, Opus 96, of 1812, which Maynard Solomon relocates in the context of the "pastoral" as aesthetic category. This novel approach to a well-known sonata enables Solomon to craft a new critical appraisal of Opus 96 as the product of a late and subtle phase of Beethoven's second period. The volume closes with the one essay that deals directly with performance issues—Mark Kroll's discussion of Beethoven's "keyboard legato," particularly the technique known as "overlegato" or "legatissimo." Surveying the sonatas in the light of keyboard practices of the time, Kroll describes many passages in which the pianists who examine the historical evidence, performance practices of the period, and the musical structure of the works can achieve effects that were quite familiar in Beethoven's era.

1. BEETHOVEN'S OPUS 12 VIOLIN SONATAS: ON THE PATH TO HIS PERSONAL STYLE

Sieghard Brandenburg

Like many compositions from Beethoven's first decade in Vienna, the Opus 12 violin sonatas (in D major, A major, and E♭ major) stand in the shadow of the works from his middle and late periods (figure 1.1 shows the title page to this opus). Although they stem from an especially fruitful and complex compositional phase, they are seen above all as evidence of his efforts to master the Viennese classical style. Certainly there are some factual grounds for this view; the sonatas of Beethoven's Opus 12 would be inconceivable without the model of Mozart's great violin sonatas—namely, the last three, K. 380 (in E♭ major), K. 454 (in B♭ major), and K. 526 (in A major). Nevertheless, they show so much individuality that it is not possible to speak of dependence or direct influence. They represent thoroughly original works of art within the conventions of the classical style.

By the end of the eighteenth century, the genre of sonata for keyboard and obbligato violin had a long tradition not only in Italy and France but also in Germany, and no doubt Beethoven had been immersed in this tradition since his childhood. As an active musician he may have already acquired a good knowledge of the repertoire while in Bonn. Two respected members of the Bonn Hofkapelle, the Kapellmeister Andrea Lucchesi and the music director Christian Gottlob Neefe, had composed violin sonatas with which Beethoven was certainly acquainted. Lucchesi's Violin Sonata in C Major (ca. 1784) is good evidence that dialogue writing for piano and obbligato violin had become generally accepted outside Vienna.[1]

By the middle 1780s Beethoven as composer had begun to come to grips with the violin sonatas of Mozart. The three piano quartets WoO 36 provide eloquent

TRE SONATE

Per il Clavicembalo o Forte-Piano

con un Violino

Composte, e Dedicate

al Sig.r ANTONIO SALIERI

primo Maestro di Capella della Corte

Imperiale di Vienna &c. &c.

— dal —

Sig.r Luigi van Beethoven

Opera 12.

a Vienna presso Artaria e Comp.

FIGURE 1.1. Beethoven, Opus 12, first edition, title page

testimony. They are widely known to be patterned after Mozart's violin sonatas K. 379 (in G major), K. 380 (in E♭ major), and K. 296 (in C major). One of Beethoven's first compositional attempts in the genre of the piano and violin duo is probably the little Sonata in A Major, published by Willy Hess, who based his edition on the autograph.[2] This work will be discussed in greater detail in what follows. According to the characteristics of the manuscript[3] and the paper used (Johnson V-A; a single sheet and a bifolio),[4] this sonata (or rather sonatina) originated sometime in 1790–91. It has come down to us only as a fragment. Thirty-seven measures have been preserved from the middle of a slow movement that probably had a three-part structure (A major–A minor–A major). The movement breaks off with the first three measures of the middle section at the end of a page, the following sheet having been lost (example 1.1). Additionally, a fifty-four-measure fragment of a fast movement, presumably meant as a finale, has been preserved. The beginning, with the rondo theme and part of the first episode, is lost. It was probably notated on its own sheet. The first sixteen bars of the surviving fragment represent the conclusion of these episodes. Beethoven did not notate the movement completely, and the repetition of the theme is implied by the instruction "Da capo." This is followed by a thirty-eight-measure episode in A minor that again ends with the instruction "Da capo." Presumably this movement was never completed, since the score breaks off on the recto side of a sheet that has sufficient space for the continuation of the movement. The piece ends with a sketch written as a single line, which probably represents a transition back to the rondo theme (example 1.2). Beethoven probably planned to continue with a further episode in A major, possibly followed by a coda.

We can hardly assume that Beethoven completed this movement elsewhere. The Sonatina, which possibly had a fast opening movement, remains but a torso. The two surviving fragments contain no hints of genius. Although it does not lack rhetorical gestures (unison passages, fermatas, general pauses), they produce a flat and clumsy impression. They show, however, that Beethoven understood the basic techniques of the classical duo of piano and obbligato violin: that is, the division of the musical material into the melody-bearing principal voice, the accompanying secondary voice that completes the harmony, and the bass voice. The main and secondary voices alternate between violin and piano by section; the secondary voice is enlivened by short imitations of the principal voice or through figuration, and particular emphasis is provided by the parallel motion of the principal and secondary voices in unisons, thirds, or sixths.

Far more skillful than the little sonata, Hess 46, is the Rondo in G Major, WoO 41, for piano and violin, which Beethoven composed in the summer of 1792 while still in Bonn.[5] This charming work is technically quite undemanding and of small scope (164 measures), but it is skillfully composed and perfectly balanced in its formal structure. The violin part is obbligato throughout, and the Rondo is a successful piece of *Hausmusik*.

EXAMPLE 1.1. Hess 46, slow movement, mm. 30–36, © by Breitkopf & Härtel, Wiesbaden, used by permission

EXAMPLE 1.2. Hess 46, fragment, mm. 1–5, 47–54, sketch, © by Breitkopf & Härtel, Wiesbaden, used by permission

   Yet another work should be mentioned in this connection: the twelve variations on Mozart's "Se vuol ballare," WoO 40. According to the evidence of the sketches, WoO 40 was begun in Bonn and completed in Vienna.[6] Beethoven published it at the urging of his friends in the summer of 1793, as revealed in a letter to its dedicatee, Eleonore von Breuning in Bonn.[7] It was in this year that he almost completely withdrew from composing to dedicate himself to counterpoint studies with Haydn. It is well known that with the appearance of the first edition by Artaria and Company in Vienna, Beethoven energetically insisted on the correct designation "avec un violon obligé" (rather than "ad libitum"), "since the violin is integrated with the piano part throughout, and because it is not possible to play the V[ariations] without the violin."[8] From the beginning Beethoven regarded these variations as "not altogether routine,"[9] and they seem to have served him for a time as a bravura showpiece with which he could outshine his pianistic rivals.[10] Nevertheless, he dropped the relatively presumptuous designation "Oeuvre I" on the title page of the first edition in favor of the more modest "No. I" when he published his first major works in Vienna, the Piano Trios Opus 1 (1795).
   A good five years passed after the Variations WoO 40 before Beethoven appeared before the public with another work for this combination, the Opus 12 violin sonatas themselves. The long span of time surely does not signify that he had completely turned his back on the genre. In 1796–97 he composed the Opus 5 cello

sonatas and the sets of cello variations WoO 45 and Opus 66 (the opus number is not authentic). As with the violin sonatas, these works necessitated confronting the problems of the duo texture. Doubtlessly Beethoven used the experience he gained from Opus 5 and both sets of variations in the composition of the Opus 12 sonatas. Therefore, these three violin sonatas should be regarded not as his first steps in this genre but as the result of a continuous engagement that goes back to his time in Bonn. By 1798 Beethoven had already put behind him this phase of technical and stylistic assimilation of classical models.

The Opus 12 Sonatas are large-scale, technically demanding compositions (especially for the piano) that are not inferior to the later violin sonatas, Opus 23, 24, 30, and 96. Only the "Kreutzer" Sonata, Opus 47 ("scritta in uno stile molto concertante, quasi come d'un concerto"),[11] takes a different path. All three Opus 12 sonatas are in three movements, following the sequence fast–slow–fast, and the opening movements are in sonata form. The expositions are expansive and consist of a remarkable number of motivically differentiated sections. The second theme group moves through modulations into the subdominant region that obfuscate the normal dominant arrangement of this section of the exposition, bringing an element of diversity to the design. The final theme of the exposition is realized in a rhetorically impressive manner. It has almost more weight than the second theme.

The first movement of Opus 12, No. 1, can serve as an example (see example 1.3). It begins with the violin and piano in unison voicing rhythmically incisive broken triads in D major (mm. 1–4), yet these figures play hardly any role in the further course of the movement. Only at the end of the development and the beginning of the recapitulation do they reappear. The actual first theme starts after the "fanfare." It is not particularly original or characteristic, but significantly the two upper voices are practically equal, interchangeable main voices. The theme, broadly presented as an exchange between violin and piano, moves to a pedal point on A and then concludes in D major (m. 27). The transitional group (mm. 27–43) begins anew in the tonic, at first with motives that are derived from the first theme and that virtually lead back to the beginning of the movement. This regressive feature is not found in the expositions of the later violin sonatas. The second half of the transitional group abandons the first theme and proceeds to the dominant with new and rather conventional material.

The second theme (mm. 43–58, in A major), presented in passages alternating between the piano and the violin, is of an episodic character. It does not form an overly sharp contrast with the preceding section and flows into a modulatory passage that merely takes up triplet motion. Otherwise, it deals with new material and is almost as long as the second theme (mm. 57–63; see example 1.4). It proceeds from A major to the submediant F major, and the subsequent concluding

EXAMPLE 1.3. Opus 12, No. 1, first movement, mm. 1–12

EXAMPLE 1.4. Opus 12, No. 1, first movement, mm. 57–63

transition (m. 71ff.; example 1.5) contrasts motivically but has little time to develop its own theme. After just six measures it leads back to A major and flows into an expanded, motivically free cadenza on E with trills in piano and violin.

The concluding section (m. 87ff.) stands in the sharpest contrast to the preceding parts of the exposition. The motion slows down to half notes and only gradually increases to sixteenths. Striking leaps take the place of otherwise predominantly scalar passages, and the attacked chords are indicated by wedges in the first edition (see figure 1.2). Moreover, the dynamic here is *fortissimo* (example 1.6). In the other themes and ideas the dynamics remain primarily *piano;* only in the pas-

EXAMPLE 1.5. Opus 12, No. 1, first movement, mm. 71–73

FIGURE 1.2. Opus 12, first edition, p. 4

EXAMPLE 1.6. Opus 12, No. 1, first movement, mm. 87–91

sage work preceding the sections of the movement does the dynamic increase to *forte* and *fortissimo,* to then fall back to *piano.*

The expositions of the remaining sonata first movements, Opus 12, Nos. 2 and 3, are not built on the same model. Rather, they feature numerous episodes and tend toward remote modulations that relax the tonal scheme.

The development sections are rather brief compared not only to examples from Beethoven's middle period but also to those from the Piano Sonatas Opus 10, 13, and 14, which were written at approximately the same time. The functions of continuing, juxtaposing, and reworking themes set up in the exposition are not strongly developed.

The development sections in these sonatas primarily prepare the point of recapitulation. The most important means to achieve this is the modulatory progression from the beginning of the transition to the return of the recapitulation. The development sections of Opus 12, Nos. 1 and 2, leap from the dominant to the mediant (i.e., A major to F major and E major to C major, respectively) and then modulate back to the principal tonality, which is reached by a long pedal tone on the dominant. In Opus 12, No. 3, the passage work from the end of the exposition is at first continued, after which the final theme group modulates from C minor to C♭ major (example 1.7). A new and strongly contrasted idea enters, a flowing melody (legato instead of staccato) that begins with a mysterious tremolo. It moves from C♭ major to E♭ minor. The development, which had begun with a stormy *fortissimo,* expires in *pianissimo.* This unusual course of events makes the point of recapitulation (*forte*) even more marked.

The recapitulations show little of the joy of experimentation. Instead they follow the conventional scheme and are largely analogous to the expositions. The deviations result from tightening up the first theme group and altered modulations in the transition to the second theme group. In the first movement of Opus 12, No. 3, the change of the first theme's arpeggio figure in the recapitulation and coda provides greater emphasis and simultaneously introduces an improvisatory element into this concertante movement (see example 1.8).

Only the first movements of Opus 12, Nos. 2 and 3, have codas. In Opus 12, No. 1, the weight of the closing ideas is sufficiently substantial to round off the first movement. The codas in No. 2 and No. 3 do not bring a new climax to the thematic material but rather unravel it in an especially witty and playful manner.

The slow middle movements of the sonatas of Opus 12 differ from one another in form. In the Andante con moto of the first sonata, in A major, we find a variation movement of great integrity and elegance. This effect results from the symmetrical proportions of the theme and the avoidance of highly colored variety or an overly large scale. The theme is followed by only four variations. The first two feature finely spun-out diminutions of the melody, first in the piano and then in the violin. The third is a minor-mode variation and, with its strong contrasts between *piano* and *fortissimo* and between legato and staccato, constitutes the high point of the movement. The fourth variation, in syncopated rhythm, to a certain

EXAMPLE 1.7. Opus 12, No. 3, first movement, mm. 96–103

Exposition:

Recapitulation:

Coda:

EXAMPLE 1.8. Opus 12, No. 3, first movement, mm. 1–5, 105–7, and 161–65

extent returns full circle to the starting point, the theme. The theme's melody is artfully placed in the middle voice (and in the bass voice, mm. 17–19). The rhythmic and melodic movement becomes calmer, the dynamics return to *piano* with occasionally interjected *sforzati,* and the last line of the theme expands into a small coda that closes the movement *pianissimo* and at the same time builds expectations for the lively finale.

Compared to the variation movement of Opus 12, No. 1, the A-minor middle movement of the A-major Sonata Opus 12, No. 2 (Andante più tosto Allegretto), is a model of classical balance. The structure is clear and perfectly regular (ABA' plus a coda). In contrast the C-major middle movement of the Eb-major Sonata, Opus 12, No. 3 (Adagio con molt'expressione), appears irregular and unbalanced. The simple and somewhat formal A theme (mm. 1–22) hardly satisfies the needed expressivity. The asymmetry of its sections (eight bars, seven bars, four bars intertwined, four bars) brings an unrest to the order of events that does not quite fit with the pathos of adagio. The following middle section (B, mm. 23–38) is built in evenly proportioned four-bar phrases, but the distant modulation from C major to Db major and back to C major creates instability in the section. The repetition of the A theme (mm. 39–46) is limited to the first eight measures of the first phrase. A long, drawn-out coda is then attached, which disrupts the proportions and shifts the weight of the movement to the end. This is further emphasized by the concertante cadence (m. 60ff.) that, in a deceptive move to Eb major (m. 64), initially avoids the tonic of C major and does not return to it until four bars later (m. 68). Thus this Adagio is an individual and experimental form that never corresponds to the template of the sentimental "Adagio" of the time.

The finales of the three sonatas of Opus 12 are all rondo movements. They follow the three-part form (based on first-movement sonata form) as developed by Mozart, Haydn, and other masters of the time, which Beethoven had already employed in his Opus 2 piano sonatas (1794–95). This sequential form allows the composer to present a greater wealth of ideas and employ greater technical skill than does the stricter first-movement sonata form. In each case there are three episodes wherein the refrain theme and the first episode form the exposition; the first episode corresponds to the second theme group and occupies the dominant key area. The refrain and the third episode correspond to the recapitulation (A'); the third episode more or less repeats the first episode but moves to the tonic key area. The middle section (B)—refrain and second episode—shows developmental, modulatory elements in the transition from the refrain to the second episode and in the return from the second episode to the next refrain. This is, however, far removed from a true development, as found, for example, in the finale of the Second Symphony. The second episode has its own thematic and tonal axes. The B section of the third movement to Opus 12, No. 1, most nearly approaches the development of a first-movement sonata form. The third movement of each sonata ends with a coda, and the coda of Opus 12, No. 1, leads particularly far afield and is impressively worked out.

From the standpoint of Beethoven's later development, the confinement to convention that repeatedly appears in the Opus 12 violin sonatas can be understood as a sign of immaturity. The forms of the movements, the themes (as in the finale of Opus 12, No. 3), and the techniques of their development are not thoroughly original but can well be called "workmanlike." The diverse motives, particularly in the outer movements, can be understood as a multicolored mosaic and show an inability to achieve a stricter, more goal-oriented form, especially when compared to the chamber music of the middle period (e.g., Opus 69, 70, 74, and 95).

Likewise, the brilliance of the figurations, the wit of the contrapuntal writing, and the effect of the remote modulations can be felt as somewhat mannered. Nonetheless, it would be incorrect to interpret these characteristics as indicating an earlier compositional date, long before 1798, as did J. H. Wetzel. In his analyses, thorough yet hardly readable today, this disciple of Riemann asserts that these sonatas fall back on compositional techniques from the Bonn period and were only reworked for the publication of 1797–98.[12] His thesis does not stand, however, as we see from the surviving sketches. Compared to his contemporaries, Beethoven was an "avant-gardist" in his Opus 12 sonatas.

So far, sketches have been identified only for Opus 12, Nos. 2 and 3—on a number of leaves of the so-called Fischhof Miscellany, autograph 28, in Berlin and a single leaf, MS 83, in Paris.[13] They obviously represent only a fraction of what originally must have existed. The verso side of MS 83 bears a draft (in score notation on two staves) of fifteen measures from the first movement of Opus 12, No. 2; on 31v–33v of autograph 28 we find drafts for the first movement (development, recapitulation, and coda) and the second movement of this same sonata in predominantly single-voice continuous notation; 46r and 46v of autograph 28 contain a number of short drafts to all three movements of Opus 12, No. 3. (The sketches on 37r, autograph 28, cannot be positively identified with Opus 12, No. 3.)[14] The surviving sketches represent different stages of composition. According to its design, the material in MS 83 could have been intended for a piano sonata. Johnson dated it as 1797 at the earliest.[15] It is a "concept sketch," such as usually appears at the beginning of the compositional procedure. The remaining sketches for the first movement of Opus 12, No. 2, correspond to the stage of "execution" (*Ausführung*), according to the categories of eighteenth-century aesthetics. This is a compositional phase that follows "invention" (*Erfindung*) and "layout" (*Anlage*). The parts of the movements are notated together and then selectively reworked. This step is usually followed by the "elaboration" (*Ausarbeitung*) into a score. The sketches do not offer any indication that Beethoven had merely taken up and revised older material.

The sketches for Opus 12, No. 3, belong to an earlier compositional stage, namely the invention and layout phases. Various themes and movement sections are notated briefly and mostly deviate considerably from their final form. Therefore, their identification cannot always be made with complete certainty. If Beethoven had merely reworked existing material, then the assignment to Opus 12, No. 3, would have doubtlessly been much easier. The possibility that he recycled individual ideas from earlier works cannot be completely ruled out. As Andreas Rücker has pointed out in his study of structure in Beethoven's piano music, a quotation in the Kafka Miscellany from approximately 1793–94 appears to agree almost literally with two measures from the first movement of Opus 12, No. 3 (mm. 115–16 or 117–18; see example 1.9).[16] Nevertheless, Rücker's speculation that the entire sonata had already been conceived by 1793–94 is too far-fetched. The musical idea he cites in Kafka is taken out of context and continues differently from the corresponding figure in Opus 12, No. 3. It consists of only conventional passage work and is not sufficiently characteristic to represent an entire work such as Opus 12, No. 3.

The sketches for the second movement of Opus 12, No. 2, on 31v and 32r of Fischhof, inscribed in an empty space, are obviously later than the other notations (see figures 1.3 and 1.4 and example 1.10). Among the earlier notations are several that distantly resemble the first movement of Opus 12, No. 1; the tonality is D major in each case. They could have been a first tentative step. If this assignment to Opus 12, No. 1, is correct, this sonata originated at a time close to that of its brethren.

EXAMPLE 1.9. Kafka sketch, Rücker, Kerman

FIGURE I.3. Fischhof, 31v, Berlin (Staatsbibliothek, Mus. ms. Beethoven Autograph 28 [Fischhof Miscellany]), used by permission

FIGURE I.4. Fischhof, 32r, Berlin (Staatsbibliothek, Mus. ms. Beethoven Autograph 28 [Fischhof Miscellany]), used by permission

a) Fischhof f. 31v, staves 5-6

b) Fischhof f. 32r, staves 1/2

EXAMPLE 1.10. Fischhof, f. 31v, st. 5–6; f. 32r, st. 1–2, Berlin (Staatsbibliothek, Mus. ms. Beethoven Autograph 28), used by permission

Using detailed paper and handwriting analysis, Douglas Johnson dates the sketches of Opus 12, Nos. 2 and 3, found in autograph 28 to the first half of 1798.[17] One can also rely on the performance date: according to a notice that survives in the Archiv der Gesellschaft der Musikfreunde in Vienna, Beethoven played a "Sonata mit Begleitung" in a concert of the singer Josepha Duschek on 29 March 1798. The accompanying instrument is not specified, but since the violinist Ignaz Schuppanzigh also performed in this concert, one can speculate that it involved the violin sonatas of Opus 12. As is well known, the autographs, which may have carried a date, are now lost. Since the *Wiener Zeitung* of 12 January 1799 announced that the printed first edition by Artaria and Company was "newly available,"[18] the sonatas must have already been obtainable by December 1798 at the latest, and the completion date was probably a few months earlier. Beethoven's first sketchbook, Grasnick 1, documents that in the fall of 1798 Beethoven had already busied himself with other projects, among others the string quartets of Opus 18.

The biographical basis for the genesis of the Opus 12 sonatas is not known. They probably do not trace back to a compositional commission, which would have called for a dedication not to a composer—Salieri—but to a patron from the circle of the music-loving Viennese aristocracy. It seems likely that the sonatas were developed for Beethoven's own use on a special occasion. The French violinist Rodolphe Kreutzer was in Vienna for several weeks in the spring of 1798 (the beginning of February until the middle of April). Beethoven became acquainted with

him then, and in 1804 he still fondly remembered Kreutzer's visit.[19] According to
the diaries of Count Karl von Zinzendorf, Beethoven gave a private concert with
Kreutzer at Prince Lobkowitz's residence on 5 April 1798.[20] Perhaps the Opus 12
violin sonatas trace back to Kreutzer's appearance in Vienna.

The public's reception of these new works was ambivalent. The negative review
that appeared in the *Allgemeine Musikalische Zeitung* of 5 June 1799 has drawn frequent comment.[21] It has generally been dismissed as a glaring misjudgment, but
this is a superficial conclusion. The anonymous reviewer initially stresses that he
is not familiar with the "piano works of the author." Given that Beethoven had
published hardly anything other than piano works before 1799, this means that
the author was quite unfamiliar with the works of the young Beethoven. He may
have known only that Beethoven was considered a piano composer. His confes-
sion means no more than that he had examined the sonatas impartially and in a
well-meaning manner. As he says metaphorically, he intended to take "a stroll
through an attractive forest with a genial friend." But he was "caught up by hostile entanglements at every turn, [and] finally, weary, exhausted, and without joy,"
he returned from his walk. Although the reviewer's judgment is negative, it does
not question the composer's talent. This is already evident from the scale of the
review, which takes up nearly a whole column. Per editorial custom, the reviewer
did not rate the sonatas as bad, but neither did he prize them as good compositions.
Above all, the newspaper reviews sought to determine the appropriate public, "lest
the aficionado, as often happens, [be] coerced into buying compositions that, even
if they are actually good, are nevertheless not [suitable] for him." "Insignificant
and bad compositions" would have been mentioned by the editors only in the
"Intelligenzblatt"—simple notices rather than reviews.[22]

Further, the terms by which the reviewer characterizes the sonatas do not question the composer's originality and artistic understanding. Indeed, he views the
works as having taken both attributes to extremes. He concedes that Beethoven
pursued his "own path," although this path is "weird," "bizarre," and "toilsome."
Many peculiarities of the three sonatas are unnatural and "forced" (*gesucht*). The
reviewer especially accuses Beethoven of "searching for unusual modulations" and
of harboring a "distaste for normal [harmonic] combinations." His ideal is apparently marked by evenness, euphony, complaisance, and accessibility. He misses
"nature," "song," and "sound method" and criticizes the "grating quality" of this
music, in which he is unable to feel an interest. Perhaps he is an advocate of the
"galant style."

The composer's technical skill is indirectly recognized, since his music appears
to be "learned." This excess is to be criticized: "Learned, learned, and ever more
learned." The sonatas are nothing but "a mass of learning." In complaining that
they are "overladen with outlandish difficulties" and "overly heavy with inven-

tion and complexities," the reviewer seems to be referring to technical aspects of both composition and performance. Following the editorial guidelines, he gives the public a recommendation at the end of his article: the three violin sonatas are "of great use as a method for piano players who are already trained." Oddly enough, the violin is not mentioned in the entire review. If a pianist "plays these sonatas with absolute precision, they can experience pleasure in the thing itself as well as pleasant self-satisfaction."

One cannot deny that this review, as rigid as it appears to be, typifies a certain segment of the readership of the *Allgemeine Musikalische Zeitung*. Similar reservations against Beethoven's music can be found consistently in later reviews. It is unlikely that the personal prejudices of the reviewer, the editor (Friedrich Rochlitz), or the publisher (Breitkopf und Härtel) have crept in here. The defensive reaction is to a large extent provoked by "the thing itself," Beethoven's willful compositional style. The extraordinarily positive criticism (9 Oct. 1799) of the Opus 10 piano sonatas is a good example. After lengthy praise of his genius, his originality, and his unusual thoroughness of the "high compositional style [*höhere Schreibart*]," Beethoven is reproached anew for his proclivity to bizarre structures and his propensity for "dark artificiality or artificial darkness." The reviewer warns: "In all arts, there is an overloading that comes from too many and too frequent urges to impress and to be learned, just as there is a clarity that can well persist in all the thoroughness and variety of the composition."[23] It is noteworthy that these reservations are expressed not only against Beethoven's "revolutionary works" of the "new path" but even concerning what we see as the "classical" compositions of the early Viennese period. This indicates that contemporaries would have deemed them not conventional and tradition-bound but fresh and new.

With all the rejections that the Opus 12 violin sonatas may have encountered, there was nevertheless a strong faction in Vienna and elsewhere that expressed its appreciation of these works. Otherwise the dedication to the imperial Kapellmeister Antonio Salieri, from whom the young, rising composer surely expected patronage, would be inconceivable. In addition, the publishers obviously estimated the worth and potential sales of the three violin sonatas higher than the critics did. Artaria's first edition was reprinted eight times within a few years: as early as 1800 by Simrock in Bonn and Imbault in Paris, in 1800–1801 by Broderip and Wilkinson in London, in 1801 by Pleyel in Paris, in 1802 by Clementi and Company in London, in 1804 by Sieber in Paris, in 1806 by Zulehner in Mainz, and in 1808 by Böhme in Hamburg. Fourteen further editions followed by 1827, among them those of the important Leipzig publishers C. F. Peters and Breitkopf und Härtel. The great response in France and England is remarkable. Consequently, during Beethoven's lifetime the Opus 12 violin sonatas occupied a central place in the repertoire.

How did the composer himself view his work? It is known from many of his later comments that the growing popularity of his early Viennese compositions did not please Beethoven. It appeared to him to be evidence of the general public's meager understanding of art. For example, he brusquely rejected orders for compositions in the style of the Septet in E♭ Major, Opus 20, or of the First Symphony, and there are indications that he had certain reservations about his earlier violin sonatas. On 6 August 1812 he participated in a charity concert in Karlsbad with the violinist Giovanni Battista Polledro, performing one of his "early sonatas with violin." The choice of program was obviously not to Beethoven's taste, but as he reported several days later to Archduke Rudolph, there was no other music to be found at the small spa.[24] Additionally, Polledro had insisted on the piece, and so Beethoven had to consent "to play an old sonata." The whole event was, as he wrote with characteristic wordplay, a "poor concert for the poor." A notice of the concert gives neither opus number nor key but merely calls the work a "Grosse Sonate für das Piano Forte, mit Begleitung einer Violine" (a grand sonata for piano with violin accompaniment). The sonata thus cannot be reliably identified, but it could have been one of the Opus 12 violin sonatas. A few months after the concert in Karlsbad, Beethoven was fully able to show how he imagined the ideal violin sonata. In December 1812 he composed the G-major Sonata Opus 96 for Archduke Rudolph and the violinist Pierre Rode.

Notes

1. Andrea Lucchesi, *Sonate facile pour le clavecin ou forte-piano avec accompagnement de violon* (Leipzig: Lehmann, ca. 1784).

2. Beethoven, *Supplemente zur Gesamtausgabe IX* (Wiesbaden: Breitkopf und Härtel, 1965), 115–18; Willy Hess, *Verzeichnis der nicht in der Gesamtausgabe veröffentlichten Werke Ludwig van Beethovens* (Wiesbaden: Breitkopf und Härtel, 1957), no. 46.

3. Staatsbibliothek zu Berlin—Preußischer Kulturbesitz, Musikabteilung, Mus. ms. autogr. Beethoven Artaria 131, a single sheet and a bifolio.

4. Douglas P. Johnson identifies it as Bonn paper type V-A in *Beethoven's Early Sketches in the "Fischhof Miscellany"* (Ann Arbor, Mich.: UMI, 1980), 256, 259.

5. For the dating of WoO 41, compare Beethoven's letter to Eleonore von Breuning in the summer of 1792; see Beethoven, *Briefwechsel Gesamtausgabe,* ed. Sieghard Brandenburg, 7 vols. (Munich: G. Henle, 1996–98), no. 4. Emily Anderson dates the letter as "early June, 1794"; see Anderson, *The Letters of Beethoven,* 3 vols. (London: Macmillan, 1961), no. 9.

6. See Johnson, *Early Sketches,* 251.

7. See Eleonore von Breuning, 2 November 1793, *Briefwechsel,* no. 11.

8. See Beethoven to unnamed recipient, June 1792, *Briefwechsel,* no. 10.

9. Ibid.

10. See the postscript, Beethoven to von Breuning, 2 November 1793, *Briefwechsel,* no. 11.

11. Accoding to Georg Kinsky and Hans Halm (*Das Werk Beethovens* [Munich: Henle, 1955], 111), *stilo* was emended to *stile* in later issues of the first edition.

12. Justus Hermann Wetzel, *Beethovens Violinsonaten* (Berlin: Max Hesse, 1924), 25. We find similar remarks in other portions of Wetzel's analyses of the Opus 12 sonatas.

13. Staatsbibliothek zu Berlin, Mus. ms. autogr. Beethoven 28, 31v, 33v, and 46r–v; Bibliothèque nationale, Paris, Beethoven MS. 83.

14. See Johnson, *Early Sketches,* 344.

15. Ibid., 342.

16. Andreas Rücker, "Beethovens Klaviersatz—Technik und Stilistik," Ph.D. diss., Univer-

sity of Heidelberg, 1999, 152. The quotation (used by permission of the British Library) comes from the Kafka Miscellany (British Library, London, Additional Manuscript 29801, fol. 161r); see also Ludwig van Beethoven, *Autograph Miscellany from circa 1786 to 1799: British Museum Additional Manuscript 29801, ff. 39–162 ("The Kafka Sketchbook"),* ed. Joseph Kerman, 2 vols. (London: British Museum, 1970); a complete transcription may be found in 2:273.

17. See Johnson, *Early Sketches,* 342.

18. *Wiener Zeitung,* 12 January 1799, p. 122.

19. See Beethoven to Nikolaus Simrock, 4 October 1804, *Briefwechsel,* no. 193.

20. Hans Wagner, ed., *Wien von Maria Theresia bis zur Franzosenzeit: Aus den Tagebüchern des Grafen Karl von Zinzendorf* (Vienna: Wiener Bibliophile Gesellschaft, 1972), 105.

21. *Allgemeine Musikalische Zeitung,* 5 June 1799, cols. 570–71.

22. *Allgemeine Musikalische Zeitung,* Intelligenzblatt, no. 1, 3 Oct. 1798.

23. *Allgemeine Musikalische Zeitung,* 9 October 1799, cols. 25–27.

24. Beethoven to Archduke Rudolph, 12 August 1812, *Briefe,* no. 592.

2. "ON THE BEAUTIFUL IN MUSIC": BEETHOVEN'S "SPRING" SONATA FOR VIOLIN AND PIANO, OPUS 24

Lewis Lockwood

This chapter's title carries several meanings. It quotes the long-accepted translation of the title to Eduard Hanslick's famous essay of 1854, *Vom Musikalisch-Schönen* (more recently—and more literally—translated as *On the Musically Beautiful*).[1] This treatise, which Hanslick described as "a contribution to a revision of musical aesthetics," may be the best-known traditional statement of the view that music's principal aesthetic value is found not in its capacity to embody feelings or to depict or represent objects outside itself but in its purely relational content, in the intrinsically musical ideas that composers shape into "sounding forms in motion." His polemic speaks on behalf of the autonomy of musical beauty.

This chapter deals with the stylistic background and profile of a single early Beethoven violin sonata, not with general principles, in the manner of Hanslick. Nonetheless, its thesis is that the special character of this work can be interpreted partly as the composer's early response to questions and feelings about the nature of "the beautiful." I aim to show that this work taps a particular vein of Beethoven's style in which he was seeking to create an object of unusual beauty and that he harnessed special technical means, derived from antecedent works by himself and others, to carry out this purpose. That he succeeded is a matter of historical fact, for the strong aesthetic appeal of this work has never failed to make itself felt by performers and listeners. Its nickname, the "Spring" Sonata, which apparently did not originate with Beethoven but was already in use by 1860, shows that listeners from early on were seeking an appropriate metaphor for the special features of this work, its consistent melodic elegance and ingratiating musical qualities.[2]

Beethoven wrote this sonata during the summer and fall of 1800, as we know from sketches for both Opus 24 and its companion, the A-minor Sonata Opus 23, which appear in two sketchbooks. The first is the sketchbook known as manuscript "autograph 19[e]," previously located at the Berlin Staatsbibliothek. Dismembered and scattered to locations as far apart as Berkeley and St. Petersburg, this sketch-book has been reconstructed in a brilliant publication by Richard Kramer, who has also brought out still another leaf of the book recently found in Milan.[3] Autograph 19[e] contains substantial material for the revisions of the quartets Opus 18, Nos. 1 and 2, and important sketches for No. 6. It also has extensive material for the B♭-Major Piano Sonata, Opus 22, and the A-minor Violin Sonata, Opus 23. For Opus 24 it holds one brief but valuable item, namely, something that appears to be an early concept sketch for the first movement.[4] A richer source for Opus 24 is the manuscript Landsberg 7, long known to contain sketch material for all four movements of the sonata.[5] Here the "Spring" Sonata emerges, with Opus 23, in the immediate context of two differently dramatic compositions—the Second Symphony and the *Prometheus* ballet—plus some early ideas for the Piano Sonatas Opus 26 and Opus 27, No. 1.

Then there is the autograph manuscript of Opus 24, probably written in 1801, which now lacks the finale but has a set of interesting improvements of details in the first three movements.[6] Finally, we have the first edition, issued by Mollo in Vienna in 1801, which offers Opus 23 and Opus 24 under a single opus number (that is, "Opus 23") but curiously presents the violin parts in two formats: that of Opus 23 ("Sonata I") in tall format and that of Opus 24 ("Sonata II") in oblong format. Since this made it impossible to bind them together, early in 1802 Mollo republished the two sonatas as separate works with independent opus numbers.[7]

Opus 23 and Opus 24 belong to an intensely productive phase of Beethoven's earlier career. In 1799 and 1800 the composer wrote the Septet in E♭ Major, the First Symphony, and *Prometheus,* a group of works aimed at consolidating his success with the public. Then turning to string chamber music for the first time since the Opus 9 string trios, Beethoven wrote the C-major String Quintet, Opus 29, and launched his career as a quartet composer with the six of Opus 18. On these quartets, written in 1798–1801, he lavished fierce self-criticism as he came to grips for the first time with the idiomatic requirements of the genre. At the same time he was turning out eight important piano sonatas, from the "Pathétique," Opus 13, to the "Pastorale," Opus 28.[8] As for duo sonatas, he followed the Opus 12 violin sonatas of 1797–98 with several new works of different kinds. One was the Horn Sonata, Opus 17; the other two were these paired violin sonatas, Opus 23 and Opus 24. Since there is evidence that Beethoven initially imagined Opus 24, at least briefly, as a solo piano work rather than a violin sonata, and since he seems to have been temporarily uncertain about the destination of certain movements, we can envision his concentration on the solo keyboard sonata and the violin sonata at this time as virtually a single large chamber music enterprise.

During these years Beethoven's first awareness of his growing deafness was beginning to darken his relations to the world around him, yet he was artistically more fertile than ever before. This paradox emerges in three letters of 1801, in which Beethoven reported his symptoms to his old friends Franz Wegeler and Karl Amenda yet expressed his determination to persevere.[9] It is the second Wegeler letter, of November 1801, that contains the phrase "I will seize Fate by the throat—it will certainly not crush me completely."[10] A few months earlier he had written: "I live entirely in my music; and hardly have I completed one composition than I have already begun another. At my present rate, I often produce three or four works at a time."[11]

There was a ready market for sonatas. As Gottfried Härtel wrote to him in May 1801, "Since you yourself wish to learn what kinds of works would please us most, these are piano sonatas without accompaniment, or also with accompaniment of violin, or of violin and cello."[12] Within his massive sonata project of these years Beethoven expanded his reach by writing consecutive works of different character in the five piano sonatas from Opus 22 to Opus 28, written in close succession. This group includes the elegant Opus 22; the Ab-major Sonata, Opus 26, with its lyrical and elegiac movements; the two cyclic sonatas of Opus 27, both "quasi una fantasia"; and the "Pastorale" Sonata, Opus 28. These works surprised the critics and the public with their idiosyncrasies even more than had the violin sonatas of Opus 12, which a reviewer of 1799 had declared to be "quite peculiar [and] overladen with strange difficulties." This critic further said that, after playing through these sonatas, he felt like a man "lost in a forest, caught up by hostile entanglements at every turn" and finally emerging "weary, exhausted, and without joy" (see ch. 1). He continues, "It is undeniable that Herr Beethoven goes his own way; but what a bizarre and tiresome way it is!"[13] The five piano sonatas of the Opus 22 to Opus 28 group were regarded as technically very difficult, despite their occasional virtues, but also as "strange and adventurous," as a critic said of the "Pastorale" Sonata in 1802.[14]

An early review of Opus 23 and Opus 24, also of 1802, was equally mixed. The critic went to some length to remind his readers that Beethoven's earlier works "had not found the friendliest reception everywhere because [they] stormed about in an unfriendly, wild, gloomy, and dreary manner." About Opus 23 and Opus 24 he had nothing much to say except that he liked their "scherzos," but he failed to discriminate between the animated scherzo movement of Opus 24 and the slow movement of Opus 23, marked "Andante scherzoso, più Allegretto."[15]

Some aspects of Opus 23 call for brief comment here. This work is the wayward stepchild among Beethoven's violin sonatas, and perhaps among all his chamber music compositions. Its primary key, A minor, is as rare for him as it had been for Haydn and Mozart.[16] The sonata opens with a Presto in 6/8 (see example 2.1), a tempo and meter that he usually reserves for finales; then come the somewhat jocular Andante scherzoso in 2/4 as slow movement (example 2.2) and a minor-mode rondo, Allegro molto (example 2.3), with extremely contrasting episodes. The finale begins with a highly concentrated two-voice theme in the piano, with filler in the violin. Its episodes include one in A major, with its curious and quirky repetitions of a two-note pattern alternating between instruments right to the end (example 2.4). The climax of the finale's coda brings back the initial two-voice theme of the movement in double counterpoint, with the original bass now in high register in the violin and the original top line now in low register in the piano left hand; the top line then regains the upper hand as the movement reaches its close (example 2.5).

EXAMPLE 2.1. Beethoven, Violin Sonata in A Minor, Opus 23, first movement, mm. 1–13

EXAMPLE 2.2. Opus 23, second movement, mm. 1–15

EXAMPLE 2.3. Opus 23, third movement, mm. 1–12

EXAMPLE 2.4. Opus 23, third movement, mm. 74–93

EXAMPLE 2.5. Opus 23, third movement, mm. 299–318

In contrast to the eccentric Opus 23, the opening of Opus 24 transports the listener into an oasis of calm and serenity. The work's four-movement composition plan is new in the violin sonatas, and its witty little Scherzo is a tour de force in the genre. In addition, the larger balance of movements is reinforced by audible thematic relationships. Thus the lyrical four-note turn motifs of the first-movement opening theme are directly reflected in the main theme of the slow movement and again in that of the finale. This is also the first Beethoven violin sonata in which a complete twofold thematic presentation is the governing principle, a procedure familiar from the Mozart violin sonatas, which Beethoven had studied attentively. At the beginning of the first movement of Opus 24, the long lyrical first theme appears twice, first in the violin with quiet arpeggiated accompaniment in the piano and then fully repeated with slight elaborations in the piano as the two instruments exchange roles (examples 2.6–2.8). Beethoven had used this procedure to open his F-major Cello Sonata, Opus 5, No. 1, but he did so there with the first, longer statement in the piano and a shorter restatement in the cello (example 2.9). In other early sonatas he departed from this model of a complete twofold first exposition

* turning figures bracketed

EXAMPLE 2.6. Beethoven, Violin Sonata in F Major, Opus 24, first movement, mm. 1–25

EXAMPLE 2.7. Opus 24, second movement, mm. 1–13

Rondo

EXAMPLE 2.8. Opus 24, fourth movement, mm. 1–17

EXAMPLE 2.9. Beethoven, Cello Sonata in F Major, Opus 5., No. 1, first movement, mm. 1–13

of a main theme, as the Opus 12 sonatas demonstrate. In those works the first theme belongs to the keyboard, with the violin as obbligato accompaniment or as reinforcement and dialogue partner. The keyboard is the primary melodic voice at the beginning even in Opus 23. Opus 24, however, is predicated on absolute thematic balance, so that equality of function between instruments governs throughout, whether in melody-bearing or figurational roles. This is one of the ways in which Opus 24 steps into a new world and foreshadows later works such as the C-minor Violin Sonata, Opus 30, No. 2, and the A-major Cello Sonata, Opus 69.

Beethoven's sketches for the first movement, disclosing his gradual discovery of the opening theme's final form, have long attracted discussion. No fewer than three scholars—Oswald Jonas, Franz Eibner, and Carl Schachter—have published analytical essays on the sketches, all of them along Schenkerian lines.[17] Each analyst examined the sketches for the opening theme in the sketchbook Landsberg 7 and drew his own set of inferences about Beethoven's procedures, but all aim at showing how subtly and persuasively the composer's changes develop and integrate the structural potential of the basic material. The first-theme sketch is already quite advanced in the first extant version; as Schachter says, "rather an ugly duckling, it is surprisingly close to becoming a swan."[18]

All three commentators note how version A, after opening with the definitive material of mm. 1–2, continues its turning figure in a rising sequence but loses rhythmic momentum (see example 2.10). In version B Beethoven improves the melodic continuation from m. 3 onward through the octave transfer and the upward-striving threefold sequence using the new figure of mm. 3–4, rising not merely to c^2 but to c^3. As Schachter puts it, Beethoven balances the initial descent and arrives "at a climax that connects in register with the structural tone A (3) that begins the theme."[19]

To these points I can add a few comments on Beethoven's treatment of melodic

EXAMPLE 2.10. Opus 24, sketches for opening theme (MS Landsberg 7, p. 17)

flow and climax, following up on the remarks of Paul Mies in his *Beethoven's Sketches.*[20] As Mies remarks, the treatment of the climactic high point is crucial for any tonal melody.[21] Having shown that Beethoven frequently prepared the way for a melodic apex by means of an upbeat, or "curtain," Mies notes Beethoven's habit of strengthening the effect of the high point by "immediate repetition of the first motive, often in a higher register."[22] The basic outline of the opening phrase is that of a diatonic descent down a sixth from the melodic 3 stepwise down to the 5, with the turning-figure on the third beat as a distinctive ornament (see example 2.6). The ancestors of this melodic design include the poignant moment of emotional recognition in *The Magic Flute* when Pamina and Tamino are reunited after their long separation. Pamina, in the same key of F major and with the same notes in the same register, offers her sublime greeting to her lover and prince by uttering his name, and he immediately replies in kind (example 2.11). That Beethoven heard echoes of this passage and of Tamino's equally famous "picture aria" from act 1 can hardly be doubted. In his aria Tamino also begins from an upbeat on the 5 and leaps up to the 3; the line then descends not to the 5 but to the 4 with an answering sequential phrase that then resolves the 4 to a tonic 3 (example 2.12). Beethoven echoes this gambit in the lyrical Allegro first theme of his E♭-major Quintet for Piano and Winds, Opus 16, a work that recalls Mozart in other and broader ways (example 2.13). These examples could be multiplied. For now it suffices to see that the character of the opening theme of Opus 24 owes much to its having *no* upbeat; instead, the opening high melodic 3 moves to the 2 and then opens up a pair of nested melodic motions as it descends to the 5, where the same process unfolds again, now at a different scale position. Thus measure 2 virtually replicates measure 1 and begins to develop its potential for generating a well-made melodic paragraph. Part of the weakness of the continuation in sketch version A lies not only in its loss of rhythmic vitality but also, at measures 4 and 6, in its use of a^1 and c^2 as resting points, basically the same pitches that served as anchoring points in measures 1 and 2. Accordingly, in version A melodic stasis is unavoidable despite the rising sequence. In version B the new energy imparted by measures 3 and 4 is reinforced when the resting points in measures 4 and 6 are altered to c^2 and f^2, both treated as appoggiaturas. Further, in the final version the sequence continues rising in measure 7 to reach its true apex in measure 8, with c^3 on the first beat. The line then descends straightforwardly and without ornament in measures 9 and 10, closing out the theme with chromatic appoggiaturas that delicately color the theme.

Much more could be said about the first movement sketches, but I want to note the terms in which two of the published analyses describe the melodic changes. Jonas has little or nothing to say about this, but Eibner notes that Beethoven's transformation overcomes the structural weaknesses of version A, and he enthusiastically continues, "How much more life there is in the final version when compared to this sketch!" Eibner values the final version for its richer rhythmic flow, greater motivic logic, and finer differentiation of the material.[23] Schachter, not-

EXAMPLE 2.11. Mozart, *The Magic Flute,* second finale, reunion of Pamina and Tamino

EXAMPLE 2.12. Mozart, *The Magic Flute,* No. 3, Tamino "Picture" aria, mm. 1–7

EXAMPLE 2.13. Beethoven, Piano Quintet (Winds), Opus 16, first movement, mm. 1–24

ing that the first sketch presents a "rising sequence that is too uniform" and that "the eighth-notes of measure 9 create a rather mechanical intensification," goes on to say that the theme's finished version "has a wonderfully fluid and graceful rhythmic design."[24]

Fluidity, grace, ductility, ease of manner—these are among the familiar terms in which the critical literature describes the opening of the first movement. Much the same is said about the slow movement, in the subdominant key, B♭ major, a highly elaborated three-part reprise form with a well-defined coda. The seventeen-measure A section remains entirely in the tonic and uses the same reciprocal presentation of its melodic material that the first movement employs. The return of the A section after the B section, however, newly elaborates the opening melodic strain and then dramatically departs into unexpected harmonic regions (moving to B♭ minor and then to G♭ major, subsequently passing from this flat-VI station to D major and D minor to prepare for the return to the B♭-major tonic—all this between measure 38 and measure 52). The coda, which occupies almost a quarter of the whole movement, has time and space for several new elaborations of earlier motives. The extant sketches for the Adagio in Landsberg 7 show that the main theme, with its twofold presentation in piano and then in violin, was essentially fixed at an early stage and that Beethoven's main task was to find the right material for its contrasting phrases and continuation (see example 2.14). Significantly, in the second of two drafts of the slow movement Beethoven shows the two primary statements of the theme through seventeen measures and then thirteen more measures of continuation, after which he writes: "etc. in G oder anderen Ton/e poi da capo [etc. in G major or other keys/and then da capo]."[25]

The Scherzo is famous for its wrong-footed humor, in which the violin staggers after the piano, always one beat too late, unable to find its place. The violin catches up in the Trio, however, and the two instruments are yoked together perfectly, only to stagger again in the inevitable da capo.

The Rondo finale resumes the lyrical and graceful style of the first movement, adding subtle chromatic inflections that are tucked into the accompanying figures of the piano left hand under the opening eight-measure strain of the main melody (the e^1 at mm. 2–3 in the left hand and the $d\sharp^1$ at mm. 4–5). Again the sketches in Landsberg 7 are instructive. The biggest surprise is the maverick appearance of a primitive form of the Rondo theme, with an F$\sharp$-minor signature but probably implying F$\sharp$ major, at the very opening of the sketchbook (see example 2.15, version A). This may have been intended for piano alone, as Schachter and Kramer note, and perhaps at that time had no connection with any sonata.[26] But after Beethoven had worked out a basic plan for the first three movements, he moved this theme into F major and began to develop it as a finale theme for this violin sonata. The main sketch versions are as follows:

EXAMPLE 2.14. Opus 24, sketch for second movement (MS Landsberg 7, p. 25)

A[1]: Landsberg 7, p. 20, staves 7–8 left (theme only)
A[2]: Landsberg 7, p. 20, st. 8–9 (alternative reading)
B: Landsberg 7, p. 32 (*36*), staff 1 (theme only)
C: Landsberg 7, p. 154 (*168*), staves 1–6 (theme and continuation)
(Further entries for later parts of the movement)[27]

Version A[1] shows the basic opening with a sequential descent from the 3 of measures 1–2 to the 2 of measures 3–4, which is retained in the final form (though with a chromatic g#[1] neighbor note in measure 2 in place of the b♭[2]–a[2]–b♭[2] eighth notes). The problem lies in ascending from this g[2] to the higher octave that is now to be reached: in versions A[1] and A[2] measure 5 begins to rise, but with a break in the rhythmic and motivic continuity for which the subsequent resumption of eighth-note motion hardly compensates.

Version B achieves a better initiation of the melody, with its chromatic turning figure in measure 2; the problem now is that of rounding off the theme at measures 7–8 as it reaches its apex g[2] at measure 7 and descends; version B seems plausible, but it turns out to be not quite satisfactory, perhaps because the harmonies it implies are not quite the right ones for this approach to a half-cadence on the dominant.

EXAMPLE 2.15. Opus 24, finale, sketches (MS Landsberg 7)

Version C, entered late in the sketchbook but perhaps from the same spurt of activity that produced versions A and B, provides what might seem an improved solution to measures 7–8. The turning figures in measures 5 and 6 of version B have given way to new forms of rising figures, going up sequentially from the g^1 in measure 4 to the apex in measure 7 and now reaching one step above the crest g^2 in measure 7 by one note, to a^2, before coming down gracefully to the c^2 in measure 8. But this solution does not last. I suspect this is because, as happens to Beethoven from time to time in his earlier years, he has stumbled on a solution for this type of phrase ending that has a famous antecedent in the music of Mozart. It is the main theme of the Rondo finale of Mozart's G-minor Piano Quartet, K. 478, in which the second phrase, measures 5–8, of an eight-measure theme rises sequentially in the same way and comes down almost precisely as in version C (see example 2.16).

So Beethoven abandons this solution and finds another, the last one he needs for this phrase. This is just one of several cases where the younger Beethoven found himself quoting Mozart, a symptom of what it meant to follow in Mozart's footsteps as a young composer steeped in Mozart's music. It is a close parallel to a situation Beethoven had encountered around 1790 while trying out a passage on a sketch leaf. He had written a six-measure passage in C minor, in 6/8 time. After looking at it he wrote himself the following fragmentary note between the staves of the passage: "This entire passage has been stolen from the Mozart symphony in C, where the Andante in 6/8 from the . . ." Then Beethoven rewrote the passage and marked it "Beethoven's own version [Beethoven ipse]".[28] Other inadvertent Mozart quotations or near-quotations recur in his sketches from time to time. As late as 1806 he was drafting early ideas for what became the C-major String Quartet, Opus 59, No. 3, and found himself writing out a theme that immediately recalled the second theme of the first movement of Mozart's Clarinet Quintet, K. 581 (see example 2.17).[29]

EXAMPLE 2.16. Mozart, Piano Quartet in G Minor, K. 478, finale, mm. 1–13

EXAMPLE 2.17. Beethoven, sketch for Quartet in C major, Opus 59, No. 3

I now return to the larger issue in this chapter—the degree to which, in three movements of this work (all but the Scherzo), Beethoven put unusual stress on melodic beauty, especially in his opening themes. The concept of beauty (*Schönheit*) was the central subject in aesthetics as it emerged in the eighteenth century as a branch of philosophy. What constitutes the beautiful and how taste and experience should intermingle in judgments of such qualities as the sublime and the beautiful had been among the principal questions discussed by writers ranging from Burke, in his *Philosophical Enquiry into the Origin of Our Ideas of the Sublime and the Beautiful* (1757), to Kant, in his *Critique of Judgment* (1790). The literature on the subject grew and intensified during Beethoven's early years, and especially between about 1800 and 1810 a number of tracts by German writers appeared. Some of these writers were loyally Kantian. Some opposed Kant's view that music, like all other fine arts, is to be judged primarily by its capacity to yield pleasure and that its value lies in its being, as Kant put it, "enjoyable rather than civilizing."[30] The opposition emerged in the 1790s, led by such writers as Johann Gottfried Herder, Wilhelm Wackenroder, and E. T. A. Hoffmann, all of whom viewed music not just as a domain of pleasure but as a means of deep personal expression that mirrors the powerful surging dynamics of human emotion. For these early romantic thinkers, music—and above all instrumental music—constitutes a unique pathway to spiritual experience. As Wackenroder put it in *Fantasies on Art, for Friends of Art* (1799): "Music is the breath of the spiritual in its highest form, its finest manifestation, the invisible stream, as it were, from which the soul draws sustenance for its deepest dreams. Music engulfs the human spirit. It means both everything and nothing. It is a finer and perhaps subtler medium than language. The spirit can no longer use it as a vehicle, as a means to an end, for it is substance itself and this is why it lives and moves in its own enchanted realm."[31]

There is an affinity between this nascent philosophical belief in the power of music and the drama and strength of Beethoven's earlier and more original works, among them the F-minor Piano Sonata, Opus 2, No. 1, and, in a different way, the C-major Piano Sonata, Opus 2, No. 3, as well as his C-minor Piano Trio, Opus 1, No.

3, and other early works in which gestural power and force dominate the landscape. These elements are always contrasted with lyrical themes and passages, as in the cantabile segments and slow movements, but with resumptions of dramatic force that were new to contemporary ears. Certainly the previously quoted reviews of his earlier works reflected the startled reactions of many contemporary listeners.

Beethoven was well aware of such reactions. Although he did not have to read philosophy or journalism to know that change was in the air, he kept abreast of current writings and reviews. Many of his works from the 1790s clearly show that he was embracing a new aesthetic that reflected his intuitive feeling for the turbulent and darker elements within a wider expressive range. He did read reviewers, however, especially negative ones, as is demonstrated by a letter he wrote to Breitkopf und Härtel not only as music publishers with whom he wanted to do business but also as publishers of a new and influential journal, the *Allgemeine Musikalische Zeitung* (*AMZ*). As Robin Wallace points out, Beethoven's name appeared repeatedly in the pages of this journal during its first years of publication, beginning in 1798. The journal's critics in these early years consistently complained about his music. One said that he was a better pianist than composer; another, that he did not know how to write variations; and still another mercilessly drubbed the Opus 12 violin sonatas in the 1798 review I quoted earlier. In April 1801, just about the time he was finishing Opus 23 and Opus 24, Beethoven wrote to Breitfkopf as follows:

> Advise your critics to exercise more care and good sense with regard to the productions of young composers, for many a one who perhaps might go far, may take fright. As for me, far be it from me to think that I have achieved such perfection as to be beyond criticism. But your critic's outcry against me was at first very humiliating. When I began to compare myself to others, I could hardly pay any attention to it, and I remained calm and thought, "they do not know anything about music." And what made it easier to remain calm was that I saw how certain people were being praised to the skies who have very little standing in Vienna.[32]

My contention is that in these years Beethoven set about composing a small group of works in which he aimed to minimize those elements within his style that listeners could readily construe as "bizarre," "ungracious," "dismal," and "opaque," to cite some of the adjectives with which recent critics had peppered their reviews. The result is writ large in a handful of compositions that stress what we have already seen in Opus 24: smoothness, ductility, ease of manner, and gentle lyricism rather than abruptness. In Opus 24 these qualities are found above all in the primary themes of the first and last movements, along with the carefully calibrated melodic beauty of the slow movement.

A neighbor to the opening of Opus 24 is the first theme of the D-major String Quartet, Opus 18, No. 3. Here the initial leap upward, from the 5 to the 4, followed by a curling diatonic eighth-note continuation, resembles material from Opus 24 partly in its rhythmic shape but even more in its legato character. This becomes more striking if we notice an alternative use of the initial rhythmic pattern of Opus 24 in the first phrase of Opus 18, No. 2. This quartet in G major begins with exactly the same rhythm as does Opus 24, with the note values halved, but continues with a contrasting dotted figure instead of the smooth lyricism of the violin sonata.

Another neighbor is the Piano Sonata in B♭ Major, Opus 22, of which Beethoven was inordinately proud. The object of his pride, I believe, was precisely the subtlety of the main material of every movement, along with certain motivic and thematic interconnections that make themselves felt in much the same way as does similar material in Opus 24. To some extent, they even entail the use of four-note motifs from the first movement that are reflected in the main theme of the slow movement and the Minuetto, while the finale's main theme is built in gently balanced, primarily legato stepwise phrases marked *piano,* reaching a melodic apex at the end through a rising motion that is reasonably similar to that of the finale main theme of Opus 24 (see examples 2.18–20). It is interesting to find, as Richard Kramer has shown, that the theme of this finale, written down in A major, was briefly under consideration for the finale of Opus 23 and that this Rondo was also once a candidate for the finale for the string quartet Opus 18, No. 6 (see examples 2.21–22). When at last it found a home in the piano sonata Opus 22, it seemed to fit into its final destination with inevitability and ease—but as happens elsewhere in Beethoven, it might have had a different goal. It is very striking that

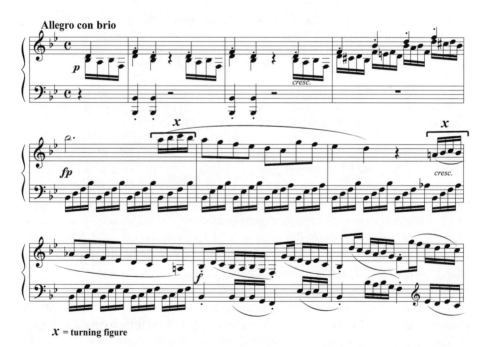

X = turning figure

EXAMPLE 2.18. Beethoven, Piano Sonata in B♭ Major, Opus 22, first movement, mm. 1–9

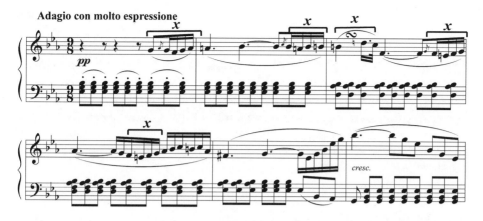

EXAMPLE 2.19. Opus 22, second movement, mm. 1–6

EXAMPLE 2.20. Opus 22, third movement, mm. 1–8

EXAMPLE 2.21. Opus 22, finale, mm. 1–8

EXAMPLE 2.22. Sketch version of rondo theme, in A major, from Richard Kramer, ed., *A Sketchbook from the Summer of 1800*, 2:87

the thematic material of all three works (Opus 24, Opus 22, and Opus 18, No. 6) makes prominent use of four-note turning motifs in sixteenth notes.

The same turning figure plays a crucial role as well in the first movement of the Second Symphony, the initial sketches for which appear in the same sketchbook (Landsberg 7) in which Beethoven was working out Opus 23 and Opus 24. Moreover, in the Second Symphony the aesthetic of gentle beauty that I seek to identify in this period appears prominently in an orchestral context, now in the famous opening of the slow movement, the A-major Larghetto. Of this movement Tovey once aptly said that "to many a musical child, or child in musical matters, this movement has brought the first awakening to a sense of beauty in music."[33] Just these qualities—legato melodic ductility, balanced phrase symmetries and sequences, diatonicism lightly touched by the chromatic, serenity, fluidity, and ease of motion (all of which are handsomely represented in Opus 22 and Opus 24)—embody a special interest in exploring the melodically beautiful, and this aesthetic quality not only formed an artistic balance to the elements of power but was a vital element in Beethoven's quest for the widest possible range of expression in every genre.

Notes

1. Eduard Hanslick, *The Beautiful in Music,* trans. Gustav Cohen (London: Novello, 1891; repr., New York: Da Capo, 1974). The other title appears in Hanslick, *On the Musically Beautiful,* trans. Geoffrey Payzant (Indianapolis: Hackett, 1986).

2. The earliest use I find of the nickname "Spring" Sonata is in Wilhelm von Lenz, *Beethoven: Eine Kunststudie,* pt. 1, sect. 2 (Hamburg, 1860), 38, where Lenz refers to the nickname as being "well known."

3. Richard Kramer, ed., *Ludwig van Beethoven: A Sketchbook from the Summer of 1800,* 2 vols. (Bonn: Beethoven-Haus, 1996); Kramer has recently added the newly found leaf from Milan, published separately as *Ludwig van Beethoven: Ein neuentdecktes Skizzenblatt vom Sommer 1800 zu Beethovens Streichquartett op. 18 Nr. 2, Faksimile der Handschrift mit Übertragung und Kommentar von Richard Kramer* (Bonn: Beethoven-Haus, 1999).

4. The concept sketch tentatively accepted by Kramer (*Beethoven: A Sketchbook,* 2:22) as an early idea for the first movement of Opus 24 is listed with a question mark and as "possibly" for Opus 24 in D. Johnson, Alan Tyson, and Robert Winter, *The Beethoven Sketchbooks* (Berkeley: University of California Press, 1985), 93 and 99.

5. Music manuscript Landsberg 7, Staatsbibliothek, Berlin; published in transcription in

Karl Lothar Mikulicz, ed., *Ein Notierungsbuch von Beethoven* (Leipzig: Breitkopf und Härtel, 1927; repr., Hildesheim: G. Olms, 1972).

6. For brief descriptions of the autograph see Georg Kinsky and Hans Halm, *Das Werk Beethovens* (Munich: Henle, 1955), 59–60; Sieghard Brandenburg, ed., *Beethoven, Werke für Klavier und Violine,* vol. 1 (Munich: Henle, 1974), viii. Unlike Kinsky and Halm, Brandenburg believes that the autograph could have served as the publisher's source for the first edition. No contemporary manuscript copy of this sonata or of Opus 23 is known.

7. Kinsky and Halm, *Das Werk Beethovens,* 57–58 (Opus 23) and 60 (Opus 24).

8. On the five piano sonatas from the later portion of this period, Opus 22 to Opus 28, see Lewis Lockwood, "Reshaping the Genre: Beethoven's Piano Sonatas from Op. 22 to Op. 28 (1799–1801)," *Israel Studies in Musicology* 6 (1996): 1–16.

9. These letters may be found in the German in Ludwig van Beethoven, *Briefwechsel Gesamtausgabe,* ed. Sieghard Brandenburg, 7 vols. (Munich: Henle, 1996), or in English translation in Beethoven, *The Letters of Beethoven,* trans. and ed. Emily Anderson, 3 vols. (London: Macmillan, 1961). The cited letters are as follows: Beethoven to Franz Wegeler, 29 June [1801], *Briefwechsel,* vol. 1, no. 65 (*Letters,* no. 51); Beethoven to Karl Amenda, 1 July [1801], *Briefwechsel,* vol. 1, no. 67 (*Letters,* no. 53); Beethoven to Wegeler, 16 November 1801, *Briefwechsel,* vol. 1, no. 70 (*Letters,* no. 54). Hereafter I refer to the German complete edition of the letters (*Briefwechsel Gesamtausgabe*) simply as *Briefe.*

10. *Briefe,* vol. 1, no. 70; *Letters,* no. 54.

11. *Briefe,* vol. 1, no. 65; *Letters,* no. 51.

12. Härtel to Beethoven, 21 May 1801, in Theodore Albrecht, ed., *Letters to Beethoven and Other Correspondence,* 3 vols. (Lincoln: University of Nebraska Press, 1996), vol. 1, no. 34.

13. Editors' translation from S. Kunze, *Beethoven: Die Werke im Spiegel seiner Zeit* (Laaber: Laaber Verlag, 1987), 18.

14. Ibid., 598.

15. Ibid., 24.

16. Beethoven's only other main instrumental works in A minor are the "Kreutzer" Sonata and the A-minor String Quartet, Opus 132. The key is little cultivated by Haydn or Mozart; Mozart's A-minor Piano Sonata, K. 311, is his principal work in this key.

17. Oswald Jonas, "Beethovens Skizzen und ihre Gestaltung zum Werk," *Zeitschrift für Musikwissenschaft* 16 (1934): 456–59; Franz Eibner, "Einige Kriterien für die Apperzeption und Interpretation von Beethovens Werk," in *Beiträge '76–'78: Beethoven-Kolloquium 1977,* ed. Rudolf Klein (Kassel: Bärenreiter, 1978), 24–35; Carl Schachter, "The Sketches for the Sonata for Piano and Violin, Op. 24," *Beethoven Forum* 3 (1994), 107–25.

18. Schachter, "Sketches," 110.

19. Ibid., 112.

20. Paul Mies, *Beethoven's Sketches: An Analysis of His Style Based on a Study of his Sketch-Books,* trans. Doris L. Mackinnon (London: Oxford, 1929; repr., New York: Dover Books, 1974), 17, 28.

21. Ibid., 17.

22. Ibid.

23. Eibner, "Einige Kriterien," 26.

24. Schachter, "Sketches," 112.

25. Mikulicz, *Ein Notierungsbuch,* 23 (= p. 25 underlined).

26. Schachter, "Sketches," 108.

27. See Mikulicz, *Ein Notierungsbuch,* 28.

28. For other examples and discussion see Lewis Lockwood, "Beethoven before 1800: The Mozart Legacy," *Beethoven Forum* 3 (1994): 39–52.

29. See Alan Tyson, "The 'Razumovsky' Quartets: Some Aspects of the Sources," *Beethoven Studies 3,* ed. Tyson (Cambridge: Cambridge University Press, 1982), 121.

30. See the translation of Kant in Peter le Huray and James Day, eds., *Music and Aesthetics in the Eighteenth and Early-Nineteenth Centuries* (Cambridge: Cambridge University Press, 1981), 221–23.

31. Wilhelm Heinrich Wackenroder, *Phantasien über die Kunst für Freunde der Kunst* (Hamburg, 1799), 146–47; trans. in le Huray and Day, *Music and Aesthetics,* 250.

32. Beethoven to Breitkopf und Härtel, 22 April 1801, *Briefe,* vol. 1, no. 59; quoted in Robin Wallace, *Beethoven's Critics* (Cambridge: Cambridge University Press, 1986), 9.

33. Donald F. Tovey, *Essays in Musical Analysis,* 6 vols. (London: Oxford University Press, 1935–39), 1:27.

3. "SONATE, QUE ME VEUX-TU?": OPUS 30, OPUS 31, AND THE ANXIETIES OF GENRE

Richard Kramer

When we conjure Beethoven in the high season of 1801–2, it is a commonplace to think of a composer at the threshold, challenging each genre on its own terms. Sonata is merely the most challenged. Fontenelle's famous "Sonate, que me veux tu?" echoes loudly here. We know this famous line only because Rousseau, in the *Dictionnaire,* happily recalled it at the end of his article on the sonata: "I shall never forget the witty riposte of the celebrated Fontenelle, who, finding himself bored to death by these eternal *Symphonies,* cried out in a burst of impatience: 'Sonata, what do you want of me?'"[1] Rousseau, writing in 1767, and Fontenelle earlier still are of another time and place. And yet Fontenelle's riddling question seems to reset itself in ever new contexts. One hears it asked, without too much prompting, in the closing pages of the so-called Kessler sketchbook, from the year 1801–2.[2] In the mere five years between 1798 and 1803 Beethoven composed all but the final one of his sonatas for piano and violin. And during that period he composed sonatas for piano alone: Opus 13; Opus 14, Nos. 1 and 2; Opus 22; Opus 26; the fantasy-like Opus 27, Nos. 1 and 2; Opus 28; and finally, the three sonatas of Opus 31, where the inflections of a new voice are manifest at every turn. Much has been written of Beethoven's little puff for the piano variations, Opus 34 and 35, "auf eine wirklich ganz *neue Manier* bearbeitet" (composed in a really quite new manner), as he claimed in a letter to Breitkopf.[3] If, on the face of it, Beethoven meant by it simply to signal the novelty of having composed substantial, original works where the predecessors in the genre were understood to constitute a lesser species—conventional sets of variations, most often on borrowed tunes—the temptation is nonetheless great to take "ganz neue Manier" to implicate the renovation of genre at every level, most radically with the sonatas of Opus 31, infiltrating to the essence of style.

The three sonatas for piano and violin, Opus 30 ("Trois Sonates pour le Pianoforte avec l'Accompagnement d'un Violon" following the title in the first edition), are the works that the Kessler sketchbook situates directly before Opus 34 and 35 and another several pages before the initial probing of ideas for the first of the sonatas of Opus 31—excepting, of course, the much celebrated one-page draft for the first movement of Opus 31, No. 2, which survives in splendid isolation among the sketches for Opus 30, No. 2.[4] If traces of this "ganz neue Manier" are evident in the closing pages of Kessler, they will not be found among the sketches for Opus 30, where, rather, one senses a relaxation within the comfort zones of genre.

Where, then, are we to locate the anxieties to which my title alludes? Perhaps here, in a music that deflects (or even sublimates) its assault on genre, that capitulates to the commonplaces of genre, where it might be said that Beethoven concedes the genre to Mozart—appropriates the model and, characteristically, eviscerates it. It is of course well known that Mozart's sonatas for piano "with the accompaniment of a violin" (in G Major/Minor, K. 379, and C Major, K. 296), in the set of six published by Artaria in 1781, served Beethoven as literal models (templates, almost) for several movements of the quartets for piano and strings, WoO 36, from 1785.[5] Further, the badly mutilated fragment of a violin sonata in A major (Hess 46)—the handwriting puts it at roughly 1790—seems unwilling to let go of Mozart's grand A-major Sonata K. 526, published by Hoffmeister in September 1787.[6] From the outset, then, these sonatas by Mozart had established themselves as powerful precursors in the canon of Beethoven's works for piano and accompanying strings.

Sketches for the Opus 30 sonatas are abundant, occupying nearly the entire stretch between pages 74 and 161 in Kessler. More than that, they are exceptional in that they have survived perfectly intact within the single sketchbook that was not vandalized in the years after Beethoven's death. Here, then, is a rare and exceptional run of sketches for a complete opus: for all the movements of all three sonatas, including, of course, the first finale of the A-major sonata, fully composed and then rejected even before all three sonatas had been completed. Recycled only a year later, in the spring of 1803, this original finale would come to serve as the finale of another violin sonata in A (but in A *minor,* despite its opening phrases)— a very different kind of sonata, "scritta in uno stilo [*sic*] molto concertante, quasi come d'un concerto" (written in a highly concertante style, almost in the manner of a concerto), as it says on the title page of the first edition of Opus 47. If there were ever thoughts of some original finale to the "Kreutzer" Sonata, they did not materialize where they ought to have been entered, on the final pages of the Wielhorsky sketchbook.[7] The evidence thus suggests that the first two movements of the "Kreutzer" Sonata were conceived in full view of a maniacal *presto* finale, this possessed music earlier misconceived as the finale of the demure sonata with which Opus 30 was to open. Conversely, the new finale for Opus 30, No. 1, composed with the entirety of Opus 30 now synoptically in the rearview mirror, must be heard to respond to the music of the original finale—although the decision to replace the finale can be pinpointed midway through the sketching for the Sonata in C Minor, Opus 30, No. 2. Any talk about "creative process" must somehow come to terms with the tensions between these two finales: together they constitute a fundamental text in all those ways in which such a text embodies a deeply histori- cal dialectic. The new finale withdraws into a saner, more conventional mode, voicing a theme perfectly under control, together with variations that behave, and with consummate grace.

Similarly, the bold, new conceptual world of Opus 31 must be understood as a response to this palpable exhaustion of genre in Opus 30. Some words of Harold Bloom, already invoked in the notion of a "precursor," get at the historical issue: "Poetic history . . . is held to be indistinguishable from poetic influence, since strong poets make that history by misreading one another, so as to clear imagina- tive space for themselves," writes Bloom in a stunning reassessment of the creative act.[8] For Bloom, the act is fraught with the tensions immanent in blood kinship and manifest in the "battle between strong equals, father and son as mighty op- posites, Laius and Oedipus at the crossroads."[9] Coming of age through the 1790s, Beethoven encounters his mighty opposite. The engagement with the violin so- nata in 1802 is a piece of this encounter, a "clearing of imaginative space"—at the crossroads, so to say—opening onto the next stage in an obscure, labyrinthine process that enables the conceiving of the piano sonatas of Opus 31.

In a passage that deserves a place in all serious thinking about how works of art are conceived, Bloom probes the cavernous apprehensions of authorship: "The writing (and reading) of poems is a sacrificial process, a purgation that drains more than it replenishes. Each poem is an evasion not only of another poem, but also of itself, which is to say that every poem is a misinterpretation of what it might have been."[10] The opening bars of Opus 31, No. 1 (and more broadly, the concep- tual world of Opus 31), may be understood in precisely this way, as a purchase on that imaginative space vacated by the taxing, meticulous labors on Opus 30 and, more pointedly, as a response to the formalities, the gentility, the suave curves of Opus 30, No. 3, as though to hear G major afresh—indeed, to reinvent it. In one sense Beethoven is engaging two genres, each with its own history, its own con- ventions and tropes, its own trajectories. Style, one might say, is a deeper hardwiring that in some measure dictates how these trajectories will go. Compo- sition activates a tension between style and genre, standing in for the larger ten- sion—for anxiety, in Bloom's account—between the composer and his precursors, even where the figure of this precursor dwells within the composer's own earlier work. In this instance, we might ponder the sense in which the constraints of "ac- companied sonata" are palpably dislodged, even whether the celebrated and bold originality of Opus 31 is in some measure a visceral response to those constraints.

Beginnings tell us quite a bit. Each of the sonatas of Opus 31 opens with an idiosyncrasy: a riddling harmony, a perverse rhythm, an isolated tone whose in- sinuation of deeper messages must be cracked like a walnut. Each makes the player think hard about the sense of a beginning, inviting us to imagine what these open- ings portend, how they are in a radical sense defining moments. The deep C♯ that sounds at the opening of Opus 31, No. 2, establishes a foundational dissonance at the outset, a leading tone initiated in the bass and a tempo-free arpeggiation that unfolds above it (example 3.1). The blatantly dissonant beginning of Opus 31, No. 3, was inscribed in the annals of theory as early as 1818, in the second volume of Gottfried Weber's *Versuch einer geordneten Theorie der Tonsetzkunst,* where, sixteen years after its composition, the implications of so complex an opening are still admired (example 3.2).[11] Famously ambiguous, the *sixte ajoutée,* as Rameau would have called it, suggests a beginning in midsentence.

The opening of Opus 31, No. 1, is different (see example 3.3). It is not a harmonic problem that is broached: no deep thinking here about tonal foundations. To call this a rhythmic problem pure and simple is to underestimate what is at stake. There is nothing in Opus 30—or, for that matter, in any other work composed before 1802—as conceptually challenging, as enigmatic, as provocative as the first sixteenth note in Opus 31, No. 1. It is of course not the note itself but its relationship to the chord that follows that is problematic. The pianist must stand in for the theorist here to contend with this relationship even as an elementary problem in performance. Is this sphinx-like sixteenth to be understood as an ill-timed, intentionally perverse *anticipation* of the first "real" beat of the work? Is it a true, highly stylized *anacrusis* to the chord on the downbeat? Is it a written-out *agogic* accent of some kind? But perhaps it is to be construed simply as a thing in and of itself: nothing more or less than a first real note on the final sixteenth of the measure. And of course one must ask similar questions about the chord that follows: does it mean to "correct" the sixteenth or simply to keep proper time? Is it "thematic"?

EXAMPLE 3.1. Opus 31, No. 2, first movement, mm. 1–6

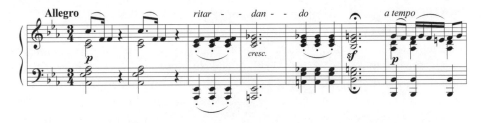

EXAMPLE 3.2. Opus 31, No.3, first movement, mm. 1–7

EXAMPLE 3.3. Beethoven, Piano Sonata in G Major, Opus 31, No. 1, first movement, mm. 1–23

Such questions inevitably funnel into a grand one of which perhaps these lesser ones are merely symptoms, a question that overrides them and that led the historian Collingwood to his classic formulation: "One can understand a text only when one has understood the question to which it is an answer."[12] This apparently coy opening then means to set off a dialectic in which all these more conventional readings collide with one another in the fleeting instant of a sixteenth note. Indeed, it does not take much imagination to understand the entire first movement as fundamentally a breathtaking and often breathless exploration of its theses. The few bars before the reprise pointedly exaggerate the problem. The pianist must engage in a delicate balancing act before the *fortissimo* return of the opening G at the reprise (indeed, it is no longer quite the opening G, which is sounded *piano* at the outset and then, curiously, *forte* at the repeat of the exposition). The chord on the downbeat is now a thing of the past, replaced by a stark reduction of itself: an octave G, deep in the bass, sets in yet bolder relief this extreme sixteenth note (see example 3.4).[13]

The only way to get a feel for this initial sixteenth note is to prepare oneself to play it. There is something about the tactile experience of the note, the tangible sensation of the note in response to the twinge of anxiety before the act, that makes the point better than can any prose, any constructed arguments. This engagement with the note is not of the kind engendered anywhere in Opus 30, where two competent musicians endeavor to make music together. In the end, the note may be heard to return us to the *empfindsame*[14] world of Emanuel Bach and to the clavichord as the crucible in which an idea of sonata evolves, where composer and performer are inseparable; where the music probes the deepest

EXAMPLE 3.4. Opus 31, No. 1, first movement, mm. 170–198

recesses of solitary imagination; where the instrument, in its extreme responsive-
ness to touch, becomes an agent of expressive thought, even the voice of expression itself. Here, for example, is some language addressed to Carl Philipp Emanuel
Bach by Christian Gottlob Neefe in the preface to his *Zwölf Klavier-Sonaten,* published in Leipzig in 1773:

> Since the publication, dearest Herr Kapellmeister, of your masterful keyboard sona-
> tas, composed with true taste, virtually nothing characteristically original [*Eigen-
> tümliches*] for this instrument has been brought out. Most composers have occupied
> themselves with symphonies, trios, quartets and so forth. And if, now and then, one
> thinks of the keyboard, the pieces are for the most part furnished with an accom-
> paniment, often quite arbitrary, for violin, and are [consequently] more practically
> performed on many another instrument than the clavichord. . . . These Sonatas are
> clavichord sonatas: I wished, for that reason, that they be played only on the clavi-
> chord; most of them will have little effect on the harpsichord or the Piano-Forte, for
> neither of these instruments is as capable as the clavichord of the cantabile and the
> various modifications of tone toward which I was aiming.[15]

It would be absurd to contend that Opus 31 was composed for anything but the
fortepiano. Still, the idea of clavichord—the phenomenon of it—must have been
deeply ingrained in Beethoven's conceptualizing of sonata itself, inextricably teth-
ered, through the filter of Neefe's enthusiasms, to the encounter with those idio-
syncratic later works by Emanuel Bach that, for Beethoven in Bonn, must in some
measure have defined the genre.[16] I further propose that we think more radically
of the instrument that in a crassly biographical sense belongs to the formative
years of Beethoven's evolution as a keyboard player—imagine how it must have
figured in his own earliest conceiving of music and how, in the purely tactile sense,
this music was brought into the physical world.[17] To play through Opus 31 is to
feel the instrument as a locus of the extremes of physical play. Here, too, this open-

ing sixteenth note is revelatory: the note is meant to grow, to crescendo through to the collapse of the phrase itself. Any self-respecting string player would articulate it this way. Victimized by its escape mechanism, the fortepiano is frustrated in such circumstances. The player is made to feel the tension between what the note wants and what the instrument allows. Beethoven writes against the instrument. It seems to me entirely plausible that in this instance (and in earlier solo sonatas), it is the clavichord, where the singularity of the isolated note can be savored, that is embedded in the creative imagination, just as it is the accompanied sonatas by Mozart, and the fortepiano for which they were conceived, that defined for him this other genre.

The beginnings of each of the Opus 30 sonatas provoke no dialectics but rather establish firm footing in a tonic, a meter, a tempo. One is not led to suspect that their author is struggling to challenge a convention, a player, a tired ear. The only movement that may have begun with the slightest inflection away from the tonic—its opening, unaccompanied upbeat C♯s fleetingly ambiguous—is the original finale of Opus 30, No. 1, for persuasive evidence suggests that the grand *fortissimo* downbeat with which the movement now opens was added later, when the movement was reheard to follow close on the cadence in F major with which the Adagio of Opus 47 ends. Rumors of the surfacing of the long lost autograph score of the finale (together with the other movements of Opus 47) persist.[18] The engraver's copy of Opus 47 has, however, survived, and it displays some travail at just this opening chord, evidence sufficient to suggest that the chord was entered by Beethoven precisely here, at this very late stage.[19] The final entry on the last page of the Wielhorsky sketchbook for the Andante of the "Kreutzer" Sonata is further illuminating on this point, for it inscribes an attacca to a subsequent Presto, breaking off on a seventh that seems to guide the ear (and the hand) to the C♯ with which the finale then opened. The sketch, in other words, seems to be working its way toward the opening of a movement already complete (see figure 3.1 and example 3.5).

Further up on this final page of sketches, Beethoven returns again to what he earlier calls "*Introduzione.*"[20] These famous opening bars are here inscribed for the first time in an inflected voicing through which the violin alone establishes the tone and in effect renegotiates the genre. Something else emerges on this final page when we hear it all as a piece. The music seems to hover about certain critical thematic intervals and pitches. Much is made of the difficult, intentionally problematic motion between E and F♮ (and all that it signifies about the transformation of A major to A minor), as a negotiation of pitch and key no less than of tempo, between the Adagio sostenuto and a Presto that begins on the minor subdominant. These are the very pitches to which the music returns in this sketch for the final bars of the second movement. Set in the bass, these thematic pitches now assume a much grander formal imperative in the return from F major to A major.

This returns us to the finale and how it was understood to begin. In these sketches for the revised entry into the finale of Opus 47, we catch Beethoven seeking to reconcile the worlds that separate Opus 30 from Opus 47, the deeply contradictory circumstances surrounding the composition of a sonata whose open-

FIGURE 3.1. Sketches for Opus 47, first and second movements, Wielhorsky sketch-book, p. 173, Central Museum for Music Culture, Moscow

EXAMPLE 3.5. Transcription after Natan Fishman

ing quadruple-stop reinvents the very idea of accompanied sonata and yet whose final movement is lifted from a sonata composed a year before this radical reconception. The layering of reversals here—of a finale composed earlier and yet made to sound as though it grounds the strident tensions of antecedent movements that were in fact composed later—seems too perverse to unpack. For however one thinks to express it, the opening phrase of the original finale was in fact conceived to follow the music of the first movements of Opus 30. Quite apart from the specificity of thematic continuity, of relationships that give at least the illusion of integrity, what is really at stake here is a deeper sense of origins and heritage, impalpable and resistant to the certitudes of analysis.

The afterlife of a work may also feed into its history. The afterlife of Opus 31, No. 1, begins in April 1803 with its first appearance in print in the fifth volume of Georg Nägeli's *Répertoire des clavicinistes.* This document contains four notorious measures toward the end of the first movement that were apparently the invention of Nägeli. (The Nägeli bars are shown bracketed after m. 298 in example 3.6.) Ferdinand Ries, in a famous passage in the *Biographisches Notizen,* describes a memorable scene:

> When the proofs [*Correctur*] arrived, I found Beethoven busy writing. "Play the sonatas through," he said, whereupon he remained at his desk. There were uncommonly many mistakes in the print, and Beethoven was already growing impatient. And at the end of the first Allegro in the Sonata in G, Nägeli even composed four additional measures, namely four bars after the final fermata:

> When I played them, Beethoven, enraged, leaped up: "And where the devil is that?" And when he saw it in print, his astonishment and rage are hardly to be imagined.[21]

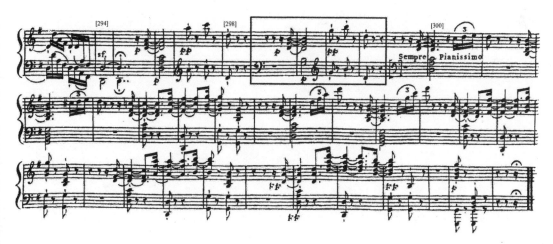

EXAMPLE 3.6. Opus 31, No. 1, first movement, mm. 293 to the end, from the first edition (Zurich: Nägeli, 1803); four measures contested by Beethoven are bracketed

The incident has been entered into everyone's anecdotal history, but I wonder whether its significance has been sufficiently examined.[22] What Nägeli, or his scribe, heard in this passage was an ellipsis, a syntactical anomaly. To have invented four bars in a work by Beethoven, even in 1803, was a willful act that must have been provoked by a conviction that the passage as it stood was simply "wrong"— that it needed editorial intervention. The only other plausible explanation would conjure an ambiguous text from which the copyist was working. The autographs of Opus 31 have not survived. In their absence, the sketches assume the pretense of authority (see example 3.7). What they convey, however, is considerable ambivalence around these very measures. After the work in Kessler, there is still some distance to be covered before the passage will be heard precisely as Beethoven wished it to be heard in the proofreading session with Ries. While we cannot know whether the missing autograph captured a residue of this ambivalence, these troubled sketches put us before a problem not yet resolved, documenting the extreme difficulty that Beethoven seemed to encounter in hearing how this passage should go. It seems to me that these sketches help us to understand Beethoven's visceral reaction to Nägeli's deed. And they call up Bloom's notion of the poem as "an evasion . . . of itself," "a misinterpretation of what it might have been." If "evasion of

EXAMPLE 3.7. Autogr. 34., Kessler Sketchbook, Gesellschaft der Musikfreunde, Vienna; transcription after Sieghard Brandenburg

itself" is understood to mean a swerve from convention, from the idealized model, then the evasion was evidently too powerful for Nägeli, who must have felt just as strongly the editor's instinct for the security of the conventional.

It seems to me that this incident and these few bars mask an issue of deeper significance. It is tempting to allow oneself to believe, as the Beethoven legend dictates, that the sketch act enabled (and bears witness to) a normative process that issued in works of greater conceptual complexity and thematic refinement, effecting unities modeled on some romanticized organicist design. Unquestionably this constitutes a part of the story. But I would like to suggest that the sketchbooks might profitably be read as the battlefield on which are played out these anxieties of evasion, of purgation, of the love-death struggle between two strong poets. Mozart is often the antagonist, but the picture is not quite so simple. This Mozart with whom Beethoven contends is not the finite, finished construction of our historical imaginations but some alter ego of the 1780s, figured by an adolescent Beethoven during Mozart's first maturity. Beethoven struggles with the Mozart in himself. To read the sketchbooks as so many road maps to the perfection of finish is to slight the deeper, unfathomable undercurrents that must underlie the Beethoven project.

In this account I have not meant to set these genres—or rather, two species of a genre—in competition with one another or to suggest a teleology in which Opus 30 leads ineluctably toward the fulfillment of Opus 31. Rather, these two groups of works illuminate the problematics of genre at a critical turn in Beethoven's career. The accompanied sonata, with its own rigorous demands, posed a problem of a certain kind for Beethoven in 1802. The intensive, indeed obsessive sketching in Kessler stands as vivid testimony to that. Again, the openings of these sonatas make the point: it is the piano that establishes the tone in each. This is not the introverted piano of the solo sonatas but an instrument that means to invite the violin into the texture. This is a social Beethoven who is making music with and for friends. There is a social aspect to the music making—and a public one (note the dedication to the Czar Alexander I)—that banishes the introspective, antisocial clavichord.

In the aftermath of Opus 31, in the spring of 1803, Beethoven would formulate a new poetics of the accompanied sonata, where the violin, from its hortatory quadruple-stop, newly controls the discourse. The duo sonata is now less about "company" than about confrontation and control. The insularity of Opus 31, the solipsistic pleasures of playing for oneself, gives way to social encounter, but scripted differently. "Sonata mulattica Composta per il Mulatto Brischdauer gran pazzo e compositore mulattico": Beethoven scribbled this outrageously personal dedication (it rings of sincere intimacy) on the hastily written autograph score of the first movement of Opus 47.[23] The movement was composed in anticipation of a performance with George Polgreen Bridgetower, the brilliant violinist with whom Beethoven would consort in a brisk social circuit in the spring and summer of 1803, a relationship that broke off, according to Thayer, in a dispute over a woman.[24] The revised, published dedication to Kreutzer, with its elevated talk of "concertante" and "concerto," has about it a whiff of respectability, of the French academy. But it is to Bridgetower, and Beethoven's brief and apparently intense relationship with him, that we had better turn for some insight into what transpires beneath the surface of this work. Fontenelle's doleful plea still sounds, if faintly. Bloom's "imaginative space," opened by the composition of Opus 30 and again by Opus 31, is filled, for the moment. The convulsions of anxiety that Bloom believes innate to the process are without end. A history of sonata, even of those composed between 1802 and 1803 as documented in the sketchbooks of Beethoven, only hints at the vertiginous depths that await us.

Notes

1. Jean-Jacques Rousseau, *Dictionnaire de musique* (Paris, 1768; facs. repr., Geneva: Minkoff, 1998), 460. The translation is my own. My title further alludes to an essay by Maria Rika Maniates, "*Sonate, que me veux-tu?* The Enigma of French Musical Aesthetics in the 18th Century," *Current Musicology* 9 (1969): 117–40.

2. Ludwig van Beethoven, *Keßlersches Skizzenbuch,* transcribed and ed. Sieghard Brandenburg, 2 vols. (Bonn: Beethoven-Haus, 1976, 1978).

3. Beethoven to Breitkopf, 18 October 1802, in Ludwig van Beethoven, *Briefwechsel Gesamtausgabe,* ed. Sieghard Brandenburg, 7 vols. (Munich: Henle, 1996–98), 1:126. For one recent study, see Glenn Stanley, "The 'wirklich gantz neue Manier' and the Path to It: Beethoven's Variations for Piano, 1783–1802," in *Beethoven Forum* 3 (1994): 53–79; for another, rather more speculative reading, see Hans-Werner Küthen, "Beethovens 'wirklich ganz neue Manier'—Eine Persiflage," in *Beiträge zu Beethovens Kammermusik: Symposion Bonn 1984,* Publications of the Beethoven-Haus Bonn, fourth series, vol. 10, ed. Sieghard Brandenburg and Helmut Loos (Munich: Henle, 1987), 216–24.

4. The page was first reproduced in transcription by Gustav Nottebohm, *Ein Skizzenbuch von Beethoven* (Leipzig: Breitkopf und Härtel, 1865), 27–28; repr. in Nottebohm, *Beethoveniana von Gustav Nottebohm* (New York: Johnson Reprints, 1970). For an illuminating appreciation of the draft, see Peter Gülke's review of the *Kesslersches Skizzenbuch* in *Die Musikforschung* 36 (1983): 101–2; for another, see my review of the same publication in the *Journal of the American Musicological Society* 33 (1980): 596–601, esp. 598–99. Barry Cooper understands the draft as the outcome of what he takes to be prior sketches for the sonata entered on later pages in the sketchbook; see his *Beethoven and the Creative Process* (Oxford: Oxford University Press, 1990), 178–96.

5. See Ludwig Schiedermair, *Der junge Beethoven* (Leipzig: Quelle und Meyer, 1925), 288–98; Richard Kramer, "Counterpoint and Syntax: On a Difficult Passage in the First Movement of Beethoven's String Quartet in C minor, Opus 18 No. 4," in *Beiträge zu Beethovens Kammermusik: Symposion Bonn 1984,* ed. Sieghard Brandenburg and Helmut Loos (Munich: Henle, 1987), p. 123.

6. The fragment is published in Beethoven, *Supplemente zur Gesamtausgabe,* ed. Willy Hess, 14 vols. (Wiesbaden: Breitkopf und Härtel, 1959–), 9:33.

7. N. L. Fishman, *Kniga eskizov Beethoven za 1802–1803 gody* 3 vols. (Moscow: Gos. Muzykal'noe izd-vo, 1962). For the seven leaves that once belonged to the book, constituting its final gathering, see Alan Tyson, "The 1803 Version of Beethoven's *Christus am Oelberge,*" *Musical Quarterly* 67 (1970): 551–84; repr. in P. H. Lang, ed., *The Creative World of Beethoven* (New York, 1971), 49–82.

8. Harold Bloom, *The Anxiety of Influence: A Theory of Poetry,* 2d ed. (Oxford: Oxford University Press, 1997), 5.

9. Ibid., 11.

10. Ibid., 120.

11. "Etwas seltener sind Anfänge mit einer Nebenharmonie. Doch beginnt der an genialen Sonderbarkeiten unerschöpfliche Beethoven eine Klaviersonate aus Es-dur mit der weichen Septimenharmonie der zweiten Tonstufe: [example]" (Gottfried Weber, *Versuch einer geordneten Theorie der Tonsetzkunst zum Selbstunterricht* [Mainz: B. Schott, 1818], vol. 2, p. 255; in English this would read: "Rather more rare are beginnings with a neighbor harmony. Beethoven, an inexhaustible [source] of ingenious singularities, yet begins a keybord sonata in E♭ major with the minor seventh chord on the second scale degree").

12. The passage, together with Hans-Georg Gadamer's response to it, is discussed in Hans Robert Jauss, *Toward an Aesthetic of Reception,* trans. Timothy Bahti (Minneapolis: University of Minnesota Press, 1982), 29–30.

13. Of four recorded performances that were heard when this essay was delivered as a lecture—by Artur Schnabel (ca. 1935), Claudio Arrau (1968), Alfred Brendel (1962–64), and Charles Rosen (1980)—Rosen boldly captures the dissonant E♭ at m. 190 on the pedal and does not release it until the resolution at the reprise at m. 194. Arrau seems embarrassed by the E♭ (it is nearly inaudible) and impatient with the movement altogether.

14. In a letter of 1768 to Johann Joachim Christoph Bode, then at work on a translation of Laurence Sterne's *Sentimental Journey through France and Italy,* Gotthold Ephraim Lessing offered this advice: "The English had no single adjective for Sentiment. For *Empfindung,* we have more than one: *Empfindlich, empfindbar, empfindungsreich:* but they each say something rather different. Give *empfindsam* a try." This is as close as we can come to an understanding of the word in the sense that I use it here. For the letter to Bode, see Lessing, *Briefe von und an Gotthold Ephraim Lessing,* vol. 3, vol. 17 of *Gotthold Ephraim Lessing: sämtliche Schriften,* ed. Karl Lachmann, rev. and enlarged ed. (Leipzig: G. J. Göschen, 1904), letter 201, p. 256. The translation is my own.

15. The translation is mine. The text is from Irmgard Leux, *Christian Gottlob Neefe (1748–1798)* (Leipzig: Fr. Kistner und C. F. W. Siegel, 1925), where the two passages appear in reverse order : "Seit der Zeit, da Sie, teuerster Herr Kapellmeister, dem Publikum Ihre meisterhaften und mit wahrem Geschmacke gearbeiteten Klavier-Sonaten geschenket haben, ist fast nichts Eigentümliches für dieses Instrument wieder zum Vorschein gekommen. Die meisten Komponisten haben sich bisher mit Sinfonien, Trii, Quartetten usw. Beschäftigt. Und ist ja dann und wann an das Klavier gedacht worden: so sind die Stücke meistenteils mit der, obschon öfters sehr willkürlichen Begleitung einer violine versehen, und auf vielen anderen Instrumenten ebenso praktikabel gewesen als auf dem Klaviere" (128). "Ich wollte daher, da sie auch nur auf dem Klaviere gespielt würden; denn die meisten werden auf dem Flügel oder Piano-forte wenig Wirkung tun, weil keines von beiden des Kantabeln und der verschiedenen Modifikation des Tons so fähig ist als das Klavier, wonach ich mich doch gerichtet" (121).

16. The works of greatest significance in this regard are those contained in the six collections "für Kenner und Liebhaber" (for connoisseurs and amateurs), published by Bach himself (but printed by Breitkopf) in 1779, 1780, 1781, 1783, 1785, and 1787: sonatas, "free fantasies," and rondos composed explicitly for the "Forte-Piano."

17. An important study in this regard is Tilman Skowroneck, "Keyboard Instruments of the Young Beethoven," in *Beethoven and His World,* ed. Scott Burnham and Michael P. Steinberg (Princeton, N.J.: Princeton University Press, 2000), 151–92. See also Richard Kramer, "Beethovens Opus 90 und die Fenster zur Vergangenheit," in *Beethoven und die Rezeption der Alten Musik: Die hohe Schule der Überlieferung,* ed. Hans-Werner Küthen (Bonn: Verlag Beethoven-Haus Bonn, 2002), 93–119.

18. See Sieghard Brandenburg, "Zur Textgeschichte von Beethovens Violinsonate Opus 47," in *Musik, Edition, Interpretation: Gedenkschrift Günther Henle,* ed. Martin Bente (Munich:

Henle, 1980), 117: "Neuere Informationen aus dem Autographenhandel besagen, da ein solches Manuskript in Privatbesitz existiert" (New information from the autograph trade suggests that such a manuscript exists in a private collection). For a convincing explanation of the rumor, see Suhnne Ahn, "Genre, Style, and Compositional Procedure in Beethoven's 'Kreutzer' Sonata, Opus 47," (Ph.D. diss., Harvard University, 1997), 97, and her contribution to this volume.

19. See Brandenburg, "Zur Textgeschichte," 119: "Der von Ferdinand Ries eingefügte Akkord im ersten Takt der Klavierstimme ist zweifellos ein Nachgedanke. . . . In den Skizzen im Keßlerschen Skizzenbuch findet sich noch keine Andeutung davon" (The chord added by Ferdinand Ries in the first measure of the keyboard part is no doubt an afterthought. . . . One finds no hint of it in the sketches in the Kessler sketchbook). In a personal communication of 1 February 2001 Brandenburg confirms that the chord, not originally present in the keyboard part, was entered first by Beethoven and then corrected by Ries. I am very grateful to Dr. Brandenburg for taking the trouble to study this passage for me. The parts, in the hand of several copyists, are today in the possession of the G. Henle Verlag in Munich. On the identity of these hands, see Alan Tyson, "Notes on Five of Beethoven's Copyists," *Journal of the American Musicological Society* 23 (1970): 439–71; and Brandenburg's refinements in "Zur Textgeschichte," 119.

20. The word at the beginning of stave 4 on page 167 of Wielhorsky appears to be "introduzi[one]," and not "mit oder," as given in Fishman's transcription.

21. The original text, reprinted often, can be found in Franz Wegeler and Ferdinand Ries, *Biographische Notizen über Ludwig van Beethoven,* rev., with supplements and notes, by Dr. Alfr. Chr. Kalischer (Berlin and Leipzig: Schuster und Loeffler, 1906), 106–7.

22. For a thorough discussion of the circumstances surrounding the matter, see Martin Staehelin, *Hans Georg Nägeli und Ludwig van Beethoven* (Zurich: Hug, 1982), 22–31.

23. "A mulattic sonata written for the mulatto Brischdauer, a complete loon and mulattic composer"; this fragmentary autograph, which breaks off at the end of the exposition of the first movement, was acquired by the Beethoven-Haus in Bonn at auction in 1965. For a discussion of it, see Brandenburg, "Zur Textgeschichte," 114–17; Ahn, "Genre," 91–117.

24. See Alexander Wheelock Thayer, *Ludwig van Beethoven's Leben,* trans. Hermann Deiters (Berlin: W. Weber, 1872), vol. 2, pp. 227–31; idem, *Thayer's Life of Beethoven,* rev. and ed. Elliot Forbes (Princeton, N.J.: Princeton University Press, 1964, 1967), 332–33. Two letters from Beethoven to Bridgetower attest to this social whirl: Beethoven, *Briefwechsel,* 1:173–75 (nos. 150 and 151).

4. BEETHOVEN'S OPUS 47:
BALANCE AND VIRTUOSITY

Suhnne Ahn

Ever since its first review in the *Allgemeine Musikalische Zeitung* on 28 August 1805, Beethoven's Opus 47 has received attention for its engaging subtitle: "Sonata—scritta in uno stile molto concertante, quasi come d'un concerto" (Sonata—written in a very concertante style, almost that of a concerto).[1] At the outset of the 1805 article, the reviewer wrote: "The addition to the title 'scritta . . . concerto' appears eccentric, presumptuous and ostentatious. It tells the truth, however, takes the place of a foreword, and so pointedly determines the audience to which this strange work can appeal."[2] For the reviewer, the mere presence of a subtitle beyond the usual dedication was worthy of commentary. Furthermore, his response, with its suggestion that the work lacked a ready audience, reflects what Beethoven must have known implicitly—that the work's unusual nature required an explanation. In other words, the final creation in some way went beyond the bounds of the usual sonata and needed a descriptive subtitle to capture the essence of the work.

This chapter focuses on balance and virtuosity in Beethoven's Opus 47. An examination of Beethoven's treatment of these two attributes should elucidate the qualities that differentiate this work from Beethoven's other efforts in the genre and also offer a key to the subtitle. I shall argue that the treatment of balance in Opus 47—specifically, the balance between the violin and piano—differs from that in Beethoven's other violin sonatas. I shall also touch on the idea of dialogue between the instruments, as well as the issue of genre—of the sonata and the concerto. I shall then turn to virtuosity within Opus 47, which demands a level of technical skill normally associated with the concerto.

First, a review of important background information is in order. The account by Beethoven's pupil Ferdinand Ries tells us much about the circumstances surrounding the first performance of the work. The first performance of this sonata occurred on 24 May 1803; there was such a scramble to get the music copied that

Beethoven awakened Ries that morning at half-past four to help prepare the parts for the performance at 8 A.M. in the Augarten. Beethoven played the piano at this performance. The violinist was George Augustus Polgreen Bridgetower, a musician whose racial background is often emphasized in the sources.[3]

Beethoven made changes in the dedication of the sonata prior to its publication. In the published version that appeared two years after the first performance, Beethoven dedicated the work to the French violinist Rodolphe Kreutzer—thus its nickname, the "Kreutzer" Sonata. According to Thayer, an argument over a romantic interest led Beethoven to change the earlier dedication to Bridgetower. As I have argued elsewhere, however, the later dedication probably has its roots in a specific work by Kreutzer.[4] To avoid the dedication issue, I shall refer to the sonata as Opus 47.

Another important point in the background is that the finale of Opus 47 was originally the last movement of the A-major Violin Sonata, Opus 30, No. 1. According to Ries, Beethoven considered this movement "too brilliant" for its original sonata, detached it, and then composed another finale.[5] This detached finale remained a self-contained movement until the scheduled performance with Bridgetower spurred Beethoven to complete the sonata.

The evidence in the sketchbooks supports Ries's account and chronology of events. Sketches for the finale of what would eventually be Opus 47 are subsumed within sketches for the other movements of Opus 30, No. 1. Moreover, the sketches to the second finale to Opus 30, No. 1, follow those that belong to the finale of Opus 47.[6]

The sources for material relevant to the composition of Opus 47 are shown in table 4.1, taken from Sieghard Brandenburg's detailed discussion of the issue.[7] As the table indicates, the sources take several forms. Sketches for the third movement appear in the Kessler sketchbook, while those for the first and second movements are found toward the end of the Wielhorsky sketchbook. Landsberg 6, also known as the Eroica sketchbook, contains no music for Opus 47, but the words "Sonata scritta in un [sic] stilo [sic; "brillante" is crossed out] molto concertante, quasi come d'un concerto" are scribbled on the inside cover.[8]

The next source listed in the table is an autograph fragment housed in the Beethoven Archive in Bonn, frequently referred to as a *Vorautograph,* or earlier autograph. This term was coined by Hans Schmidt in 1969, and although the term presents a number of problems, it has been accepted as a viable concept in Beethoven scholarship.[9] This fragment, which is in Beethoven's handwriting and in score format, contains the exposition for the first movement. Of special interest is the attribution in Beethoven's handwriting at the top of the page: "Sonata mulattica Composta per il Mulatto Brischdauer gran pazzo e compositore mulattico" (a mulattic sonata written for the mulatto Brischdauer, a complete loon and mulattic composer; see figure 4.1).

Evidence suggests that another, more complete autograph once existed. It is reported to have been in the possession of a collector in St. Louis, Missouri, but its whereabouts are unknown.[10]

Table 4.1. Sources

	Location	Call Number	Page/Folio Number
Sketchbooks			
Kessler	Vienna	Gdm (A 34) SV 263	Pp. 88–107[a]
Wielhorsky	Moscow	SV 343	Pp. 166–73[b]
Stray leaves	Modena	Campori Collection	
	Bonn	Bodmer Collection Mh 70	
Eroica (Landsberg 6)	Krakow	SV 60	Inside back cover
Autographs			
"Vorautograph"	Bonn	NE 86; SV 543	Pp. 1–12
Autograph?	St. Louis	Private possession	
Engraver's copy	Munich	G. Henle Verlag	Pp. 1–117
Editions			
Simrock (2)	Bonn (2 versions)	Beethoven Archive	
	New York	N.Y. Pierpont Morgan Library	
	Cambridge, Mass.	Houghton Library, Harvard	
Birchall	London	British Public Library	

a. Ludwig van Beethoven, *Keßlersches Skizzenbuch,* ed. Sieghard Brandenburg, 2 vols. (Bonn, 1976 and 1978). The edition consists of transcription, facsimile, and commentary.

b. Natan Fishman, ed., *Kniga eskizov Beethoven za 1802–1803 gody,* 3 vols. (Moscow, 1962). The edition consists of transcription, facsimile, and commentary.

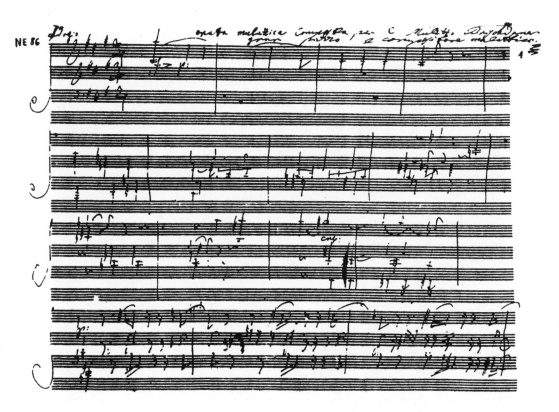

FIGURE 4.1. Autograph fragment bearing Bridgetower's name; used by permission of Peter Henle

Also surviving is the *Stichvorlage,* or printer's copy, which was sent to the publisher as the model to be engraved. This manuscript contains parts for each instrument but no score. It is not in Beethoven's hand and in fact shows the hands of three different copyists. The state of the parts for the finale further supports Ries's account that this movement was originally written for another work. Finally, the source table lists several early editions, among them the first, released by Simrock in 1805 and another early edition published shortly afterward by Birchall in London.

Balance is one of the basic aesthetic principles underlying the music of the late eighteenth and early nineteenth centuries. If we equate it with symmetry, then we find manifestations of it on a small scale in phrase length and periodicity and on a larger scale in the overall structure of the sonata.

Beethoven was acutely aware of the implications of balance in his compositions. For example, Ferdinand Ries reported that Beethoven considered the final movement "too brilliant" for its original sonata. This attitude reflects Beethoven's concerns about issues of length, balance, and proportion. Figure 4.2 contains several items relevant to the final version of Opus 30, No. 1. First is an outline of the sonata's first movement. Immediately below is the first-movement thematic incipit from Kinsky and Halm's thematic index of Beethoven's works. Next is an outline of the final version of the last movement, followed by its thematic incipit. Each outline indicates the total number of measures in the relevant movement. Thus in the final version of Opus 30, No. 1, Beethoven concluded the work with 237 measures of theme and variations, balancing the 249 measures of the first movement.[11]

Figure 4.3 provides an outline of the last movement of Opus 47 and its thematic incipit. Written in sonata form, the movement contains 539 measures. If Beethoven had used this long movement as the finale to Opus 30, No. 1, the sonata would have become decidedly lopsided—bottom heavy, as it were—and unbalanced.

Since the finale to Opus 47 was composed before the other movements, information on it is placed above that for the first movement. Included here are the first four measures of the slow introduction marked Adagio sostenuto, followed by the opening of the exposition beginning in measure 19; an outline of the first movement appears above the incipits. Knowing the order in which these two movements were written affects one's understanding of the work as a whole, for as in another work from this period, the *Eroica* Symphony, the finale generates most of the ideas for the entire work. In other words, the first two movements were written with the ending already in mind.[12]

In Opus 47 the first movement, with its 599 measures, easily balances the 539 measures of the finale. Both movements are marked presto, an unusual choice of tempo for Beethoven in any period. The codas of both movements contain a sudden change to adagio for a recollection of the first theme.

Outline of First Movement, Allegro (249 measures)

exposition mm. 1–82	development 83–149	recapitulation 150–234	coda 234–249
1P 1S I $\Rightarrow$ V m. 1 m. 34		1P 1S I $\Rightarrow$ I m. 150 m. 187	

\# of measures in each section

| 82 | 67 | 85 | 16 |

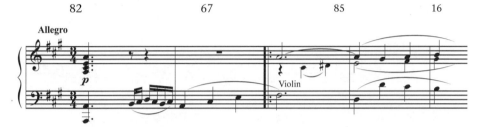

Outline of Last Movement, Allegretto con Variazioni (237 measures)

Theme mm. 1–32	var. 1 33–48	var. 2 49–64	var. 3 65–80	var. 4 81–96	var. 5 97–151 (with Adagio)	var. 6 152–237

FIGURE 4.2. Beethoven, Violin Sonata in A Major, Opus 30, No. 1

Outline of Last Movement, Finale (539 measures)

exposition mm. 1–177	development 178–290	recapitulation 291–454	coda 455–539
1P 1S 1K I ⟹ V ⟹ V m. 1 m. 34 m. 62		1P 1S 1K I ⟹ I ⟹ I m. 150 m. 187 m. 429	"Adagio" mm. 489–492, 497–500

\# of measures in each section

| 117 | 133 | 164 | 85 |

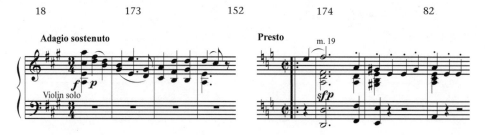

Outline of First Movement, Adagio sostenuto; Presto (599 measures)

slow intro mm. 1–18	exposition 19–191	development 192–343	recapitulation 344–517	coda 518–599
	1P 1S 1K i? ⟹ V ⟹ V m. 19 m. 91 m. 144	false recap iv- d minor m. 324	1P 1S 1K i ⟹ I ⟹ i m. 344 m. 412 m. 465	"Adagio" mm. 575–582

\# of measures in each section

| 18 | 173 | 152 | 174 | 82 |

FIGURE 4.3. Beethoven, Violin Sonata in A Major, Opus 47 ("Kreutzer")

An A-major chord spanning four octaves occurs at the beginning of the finale and at measure 5 of the slow introduction. In this instance, however, the third movement did not generate this idea for the first movement. The A-major chord in the last movement was a late addition, written after the first movement was composed, as the engraver's copy makes clear (see figure 4.4). All but the first chord is written in the hand of Beethoven's long-time copyist Wenzel Schlemmer. The A-major chord is in the hand of Ferdinand Ries—presumably at the instruction of Beethoven. Ries made one attempt to squeeze the chord in here and then used the "Vide" sign to show that the notes on the fourth system should be moved to the top. The A-major chord is an obvious link between the outer movements, made at a very late stage of composition.

The last and the first movements share a common structural feature, namely, the delay of the tonic cadence in the exposition.[13] Although the two movements achieve this delay by different means, its use in both contributes significantly to the expansion of the exposition sections from within, so to speak. Consequently, the expansion of the other parts of the sonata form helps explain the huge size of both outer movements.

The aesthetic of balance applies as well to the performing forces of violin and

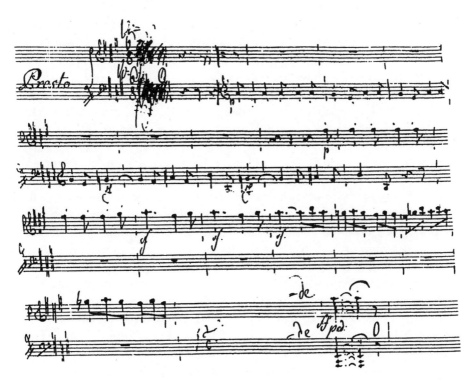

FIGURE 4.4. Engraver's copy of the finale of Opus 47, Beethoven-Haus Bonn, Collection H. C. Bodmer, used by permission

piano. Recall the subtitle, with its double reference to genres other than the sonata: concertante and concerto. The term *concertante* is not usually associated with the sonata, and its use in Opus 47 is unique among all Beethoven's sonatas, solo or accompanied.

Heinrich Christoph Koch, with whose writings Beethoven may have been familiar, makes a distinction between concertante and obbligato.[14] According to Koch, *concertante* describes "those parts of a composition that alternate with the solo part in presenting the melody, or that appear between the solo sections with soloistic passages, somewhat in order to compete among themselves or the solo part." *Obbligato* refers to "instruments that accompany or flesh out a composition" and "are heard only occasionally."[15]

The distinction is suggestive for Beethoven's choice of this term. Opus 47 marks a departure from Beethoven's previous practice concerning the roles of the piano and violin and constitutes a turning point in the manner in which Beethoven viewed the obbligato instrument.

In the eighteenth century the obbligato instrument was subordinate to the piano. About the violin sonata in particular, William Newman writes, "The violin, which had dominated during the basso continuo era, was subordinated to the clavier for at least half a century."[16] As Newman further asserts, Mozart's sonatas for violin and piano were the first to put the violin and piano on more "equal footing."[17]

The elevation of the obbligato instrument from subordinate to equal (or more balanced) status is also suggested by title pages of the first editions of Beethoven's published accompanied sonatas (see table 4.2).

Noteworthy is the shift in preposition from *with* (*avec* or *con*) to *and* (*ed* or *et*) beginning with Opus 47. Thus the title page in Opus 5, Nos. 1 and 2, reads, "pour le Clavecin ou Piano=Forte, avec un Violoncelle obligé"; and in Opus 12, Nos. 1–3, "per il Clavicembalo o Forte-Piano con un Violino." From Opus 47 through to Opus 102, however, the title pages uniformly describe their contents as works for keyboard *and* another instrument.

This change in terminology helps elucidate the term *concertante* as applied to Opus 47. Although Beethoven retained the word *obbligato* in the subtitle, he added the description "scritta in uno stile concertante." Viewed in the context of the broad progression of Beethoven's titles for accompanied sonatas, Opus 47 is a watershed marking the equal status of the participants. This new equality is borne out in all that has been said and written about the extreme virtuosity of the violin part.[18] In this sonata the violin is much more than an accompanying instrument "obligated" to fill out the texture of the work. It is given full and equal status with the piano part.

I turn now to the issue of dialogue between the two participants and ask whether there is a more viable concept of dialogue than that proposed by Owen Jander, who asserted that two contrasting rhythmic patterns serve as a kind of argument or dialogue permeating all three movements of Opus 47.[19]

Table 4.2. Partial Contents of First-Edition Title Pages, Arranged Chronologically

"With" (1797–1803)	"And" (1805–17)
Opus 5, Nos. 1 and 2 DEUX GRANDES SONATES, pour le Clavecin ou Piano=Forte avec un violoncelle obligé Composées, et Dediées A Sa Majesté FREDERIC GUILLAUME II ROI DE PRUSSE	**Opus 47** SONATA per il Piano-forte ed un Violino obligato scritta in uno stilo [*sic*] molto concertante quasi come d'un concerto Composta e dedicata al suo amico R. KREUZER. Membro del Conservatorio di Musica in Parigi primo Violino dell'Academia delle Arti, a della Camera imperiale.
Opus 12, Nos. 1–3 TRE SONATE, per il Clavicembalo o Forte-Piano con un Violino Composte e Dedicate al Sigr. Antonio Salieri primo Maestro di Capella della Corte Imperiale di Vienna &c. &c.	
Opus 17 SONATE pour le Forte-piano avec un Cor, oû Violoncelle composée et dediée A Madame la Baronne de Braun	**Opus 69** Grande Sonate pour Pianoforte et Violoncelle composée et dédiée à Monsieur le Baron de Gleichenstein
Opus 23 and 24 Deux sonates pour le Piano Forte avec un Violon composées et dediées A Monsieur le Comte Maurice de Fries Chambellan de S.M.J. & R	**Opus 96** SONATE für Piano=Forte und Violin Sʳ. Kaiserl. Hoheit dem durchlauchtigsten Prinzen RUDOLPH ERHERZOG VON OESTERREICH & & & in tiefer Ehrurcht zugeeignet
Opus 30, Nos. 1–3 TROIS SONATES pour le Pianoforte avec l'Accompagnement d'un Violon composées et dediées à Sa Majesté ALEXANDRE I, Empereur de toutes les Russies	**Opus 102, Nos. 1 and 2** Deux Sonates POUR LE Pianoforte et Violoncelle composées par . . .

In the solo concerto the essence of dialogue is obviously derived from the stark contrast between soloist and orchestra. The drama lies partly in the contrast of instrumental timbre and partly in the exchange of thematic material between the performing forces. Typically a passage in the orchestra is subsequently realized by the soloist in a manner idiomatic to the solo instrument. The subtle differences between the two iterations of a theme are fundamental to concerto dialogue. A textbook example, in which the soloist presents and varies thematic material originally given by the orchestra, is the first movement of Mozart's Piano Concerto in A Major, K. 488, often cited as an example of a double exposition.[20] After the first orchestral tutti (mm. 1–66) the piano enters with the theme initially presented by the orchestra. Subtle differences immediately appear, however, particularly in the accompaniment; an Alberti bass in the piano left hand idiomatically realizes the lower-register accompanimental instruments in the opening measures of the orchestral tutti. Another instance occurs after the second theme of the solo exposition, in which the piano, in idiomatic broken octaves, replicates the melodic line contained in the flutes, bassoons, and first violins. Thus differences in instrumental timbre are highlighted by the idiomatically differentiated presentation of similar themes or accompanying figures.

In Beethoven's violin sonatas, as in Mozart's, thematic exchange in itself is hardly unusual. His accompanied sonatas are rich in examples of thematic interplay between the instruments. Early in the first movement of Opus 12, No. 2, for example, the violin repeats a theme first presented by the piano, doing so in the same register; in Opus 30, No. 2, the opening theme in the piano in measures 1–4 is repeated by the violin in measures 8–12, now an octave higher and with the piano in the lower register (see examples 4.1–4.3). Thematic exchange is handled innovatively in Opus 47, especially in the first movement. Here Beethoven dramatizes the timbre change between violin and piano by deliberately altering the thematic material rather than literally repeating themes between the participants. The absence of literal repetition between the two instruments is striking,[21] and what takes its place can aptly be called dialogue. Not repetition but rather question and answer—or better yet, statement and response—emerges as the ruling principle. Moreover, the violin initiates these dialogues, for the most part, as in the first movement's slow introduction, exposition, recapitulation, and coda.

Beethoven alters the responsive patterns of the instrument in a number of ways, most obviously and effectively through mode alteration. This occurs in two important places. The first is in the opening measures of the slow introduction (example 4.4). The violin, playing without accompaniment, creates a rich texture using quadruple-, triple-, and double-stops. The upper line begins with descending thirds within the key of A major. The piano then responds with a melody that closely resembles the violin statement but with the lowered sixth scale degree of A minor.

The piano's surprising response by means of the modal change immediately establishes the two instruments in opposition and foreshadows a tonal ambigu-

EXAMPLE 4.1. Beethoven, Violin Sonata in A Major, Opus 12, No. 2, first movement, mm. 1–4 and 17–18

EXAMPLE 4.2. Beethoven, Violin Sonata in C Minor, Opus 30, No. 2, first movement, mm. 1–4

EXAMPLE 4.3. Opus 30, No. 2, first movement, mm. 9–10

EXAMPLE 4.4. Opus 47, first movement, mm. 1–7

ity that recurs throughout the movement. The violin's role as the initiator is immediately apparent.

Another instance of mode alteration in the first movement occurs in the second theme group. As in the opening measures, the violin plays the whole-note second theme in the dominant key of E major at measures 91–105; the piano responds at measures 107–16 with an altered version of the second theme in E minor (see example 4.5). Indeed, an absence of thematic repetition is apparent throughout the first movement. In measures 19–36 the "response" to the initial statement appears to be a repetition but is then extended to differentiate it from the previous statement (example 4.6). The Presto begins in measure 19, and again the violin has the new theme first. The piano responds in measure 28 with a theme that duplicates the violin theme until the end of the phrase (m. 36), at which point

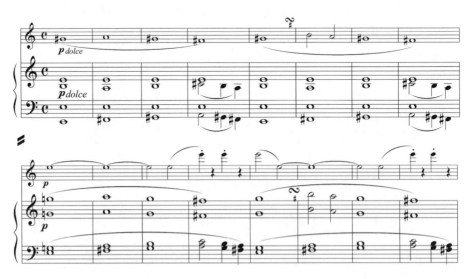

EXAMPLE 4.5. Opus 47, first movement, mm. 91–98 and 107–14

EXAMPLE 4.6. Opus 47, first movement, mm. 19–36

the piano embarks on a florid arpeggio. Here Beethoven emphasizes the opposition of instruments in a different manner, a form of "one-upmanship"[22] that again highlights their interplay and lack of literal repetition.

Still another type of exchange in which the thematic material is embellished by the respondent occurs just after the presentation of the second theme in both modes. In measures 117–18 the violin plays a short theme that is rhythmically identical to the opening measure of the Presto. The piano's "response" in measures 119–20 uses the same pitch classes as its primary structural notes but is disguised in a virtuosic arpeggiation of eighth notes (example 4.7). The result is a gesture resembling the opening of the Presto in which the piano, by avoiding repetition, appears to offer a "retort" to the violin.

Although the violin tends to introduce new thematic ideas throughout the exposition of the first movement, there is a change of roles at measure 144, where the piano presents new material (example 4.8). In measure 156 the violin answers,

EXAMPLE 4.7. Opus 47, first movement, mm. 117–20

EXAMPLE 4.8. Opus 47, first movement, mm. 143–62

and although the violin's response is almost a repetition, an extension of the melody at measure 168 differentiates it from its first presentation. Moreover, the violin's response is altered greatly by the piano left hand. While it seems the violin is about to repeat the melody presented by the piano in measure 144, Beethoven places the melody in the piano's bass range and offsets the theme by a half-measure to create a momentary stretto effect. In this passage, therefore, Beethoven once again avoids repetition in the exchange of thematic material but does so in a manner different from the techniques employed in the previous examples.

The previous examples all come from the slow introduction and exposition of the first movement. Until measure 144, as I have shown, the violin presents new thematic ideas that the piano then alters in some way. When the piano becomes the initiator, toward the end of the exposition, it interrupts the violin's response, thus creating a more animated exchange.

Except in one case, all the passages cited from the exposition recur in the recapitulation. The modal alteration of the second theme group in measures 91–116 is mirrored in measures 412–37, the elaboration of measures 117–56 is duplicated in measures 437–63, and the stretto effect of measures 156–60 is paralleled in measures 477–81.[23] The one passage that differs considerably from its counterpart in the recapitulation is the very beginning of the exposition at the Presto (example 4.9). Measures 19ff. do not recur; instead, a false recapitulation takes place in measure 324. The half-step motive originally between the pitches E and F in the exposition is now presented between the pitches A and Bb, and whereas the violin began the Presto in the exposition, the piano starts the false recapitulation. It is the violin, however, that ultimately leads to a true recapitulation in the proper key area in measure 344. Measures 345–55 then proceed very much like measures 19–27.

A sort of reversal of leading roles thus takes place between exposition and recapitulation. At the beginning of the exposition, the violin initiates a theme that is followed by the piano attempting to "outshine" the violin in measure 36. In the false recapitulation the piano begins in the "wrong key" but is led to the correct key by the violin. Furthermore, the recapitulation omits the florid arpeggiation of measure 36, presenting instead a rapid exchange of material between piano and violin in measures 354–63. To invoke the idea of dialogue, the two instruments seem to be engaged in a heated debate.

If the previously discussed material represents a pinnacle of conflict between the two instruments in the first movement, then the Adagio that begins the coda at measure 575 serves as a point of resolution or reconciliation (example 4.10). The exposition's original half-step motive between E and F appears in measures 574–75. In the exposition the F is harmonized with a D-minor chord. At measure 575, however, the F is harmonized with a more placid F major. The melodic contour of measure 19 is preserved in measures 578–79, but the rhythm is augmented to whole notes to resemble that of the second theme. Thus the passage is reminiscent of both the first theme (beginning at m. 19) and the second theme (beginning at m. 91). In measure 579 the piano enters with an altered version of the passage

EXAMPLE 4.9. Opus 47, first movement, mm. 324–63

EXAMPLE 4.10. Opus 47, first movement, mm. 574–82

initiated by the violin. The melodic contour and the rhythm are maintained, but as in all previous examples, the response differs from the initial statement in such a way as to highlight the contrast of the two instruments.

The passages examined reveal a pattern by which Beethoven introduces a novel dynamic between the participating instruments in the accompanied sonata. Specifically, he brings to the sonata a dynamic adapted from the concerto, or concertante, in which a continuing dialogue emerges as performing forces vie for dominance or, one might say, individuality of effect. Opus 47 is thus, in a sense, a concerto for violin and piano. By seeing Opus 47 as the work in which a concerto-like "dialogue" between the violin and piano is first achieved in Beethoven's accompanied sonatas, it becomes possible to view the piece as the composer's break from the norms of the genre itself.

After Opus 47, which elevates the genre of accompanied sonata to a new plane, Beethoven composed only one more sonata for violin and piano, Opus 96, although he composed three sonatas for piano and violoncello after Opus 47—Opus 69 and Opus 102, Nos. 1 and 2. It is as though Opus 47, as the penultimate sonata for violin and piano, approached the limits of one genre, whereas Beethoven still had fertile ground to seek in the sonatas for piano and cello—with the lower register of the cello and the newfound equality between the participating instruments established in Opus 47.

What emerges as an innovation in Opus 47 provides clues about the way Beethoven viewed the genre of the concerto and what he may have been attempting to achieve in works in that category.

Virtuosity, an essential component of a concerto, is also a fundamental ingredient in Opus 47. Recall the second half of Beethoven's subtitle, "quasi come d'un concerto," or "something like a concerto." This work requires exceptional technique and facility from both piano and violin. The pianist must sustain power and speed—especially in the turbulent transitional passages of the first movement exposition and recapitulation—and faces a fiendishly difficult section of thirds and sixths in the development. The violinist must execute double-, triple-, and quadruple-stops, along with fiery string crossing that severely tests the player's technique.

One aspect of virtuosity that deserves special attention here is register. Example 4.11 shows the solo violin part in measures 159–63 of the Violin Concerto fragment WoO 5. Although a sustained a^1 is essentially achieved in the string crossing in measure 159, the pitches on the E string reach a^3, b^3, and c^4.

In the Violin Concerto, Opus 61, Beethoven uses register to differentiate the solo violin from the rest of the orchestra, employing notes at or above a^3 throughout all three movements of the work. This is especially evident in the early measures of the violin entrance, where the solo violin first plays the opening theme from the orchestral tutti (example 4.12); the material occupies a range reflecting what Boris Schwarz described as Beethoven's "predilection for the silver high register of the E string."[24] The violin rarely ventures beyond a g^3 in the sonatas for violin and piano written before Opus 47, the one exception being measure 157 in the last movement of Opus 30, No. 2, when the violin plays a quarter-note $a\flat^3$ (the enharmonic equivalent of $g\sharp^3$). In the first and second movements of Opus 47, however, journeys into the higher registers and (more difficult) positions of the violin are frequent. In the first movement a^3s appear in measures 140–42. Later in the recapitulation, in measures 456 and 495, $b\flat^3$ and even c^4s appear in the violin part. In the second movement, in measures 88–89 and 107–8, the violin reaches pitches from a^3 to f^4.

EXAMPLE 4.11. Beethoven, Violin Concerto in C Major, WoO 5, fragment, mm. 159–63

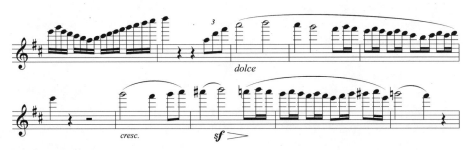

EXAMPLE 4.12. Beethoven, Violin Concerto in D Major, Opus 61, first movement, mm. 100–109

Opus 47 also served Beethoven as a bridge between the C-minor Piano Concerto, Opus 37, and the G-major Piano Concerto, Opus 58. The source material links the earlier of the two concertos with Opus 47 and further substantiates their compositional proximity; that is, sketches for the cadenza to the first movement of Opus 37 are contained on the detached leaves of the Wielhorsky sketchbook. More recently, Leon Plantinga has contributed to a revision of the compositional date of Opus 37.[25] That Opus 47, which could be considered a "hybrid" sonata-concerto, was composed within the same period as Opus 37 and Opus 58 is not surprising, particularly considering William Drabkin's claim that the two concertos represent a blending of genres. In an article entitled "Towards the 'Symphonic Concerto' of the Middle Period," Drabkin refutes "the tradition of viewing the Third Concerto as an early work . . . [and] the Fourth as a product of the "heroic period."[26] Instead, he argues, "the Third and Fourth Concertos show Beethoven reconciling basic concerto principles with symphonic development."[27] It is thus striking to consider a hybrid of sonata and concerto standing between two works regarded as a blending of concerto and symphony.

Finally, let us look at Opus 47 as a precursor to Opus 58. Michael Roeder writes: "The opening of the Fourth Piano Concerto is at once startling, in the context of the history of the concerto, and tranquil. We are startled by the utterance of the first sound by the solo instrument, unaccompanied. The piano presents the gentle, opening, cantabile five-bar phrase. . . . Beethoven completely isolates the soloist in this daring opening, creating a dramatic gesture of enormous consequences."[28]

Beethoven's Fourth Piano Concerto, together with the Fifth Piano Concerto ("Emperor"), Opus 73, is often cited as a pivotal work heralding the age of the romantic piano concerto, including Schumann's Opus 54, Grieg's Piano Concerto, or Brahms's Opus 83. One prominent feature that binds all these works is the presence of the piano solo in the early opening measures of the first movement. The soloist's elevated presence at the beginning of the romantic piano concerto to some extent represents or embodies the emerging romantic concept of the individual as a force—an idea that was to permeate many aspects of nineteenth-century artistic achievement. Within this scheme the piano concerto, with its competing performing forces of pianist against orchestra, serves as a metaphor for the struggle between the individual and society.[29] Beethoven's Opus 58 reverses the dominant and subordinate roles applied to the solo piano in relation to the orchestra. With its opening measures of the slow introduction—four measure of the solo violin followed by four measure of the solo piano—Opus 47 presages the striking opening of Opus 58.

Prior to Opus 47 Beethoven adhered to most of the traditional conventions associated with the violin sonata, particularly in his manner of opening the first movement and thus the entire work. Previous violin sonatas began either with the violin and piano together or with the piano followed by the violin. Similarly piano concertos began with an extended orchestra tutti followed by the entrance of the piano solo somewhat later. Opus 47 is the first to invert that pattern, in that the previously subordinate participant—the violin obbligato—is elevated. In Opus 47 a new dynamic was created between the violin and piano. In turn, a reciprocal influence resulted as Beethoven, in Opus 58, further dramatized the relationship of the performing forces.

Notes

1. On *stilo* and *stile* see p. 22, n. 11, to this volume.

2. The German text, which originally appeared in the *Allgemeine Musikalische Zeitung,* 28 August 1805, cols. 769ff., runs as follows: "Der Zusatz auf dem Titel: scritta—concerto, scheint wunderlich, anmassend und prahlerisch; er sagt aber die Wahrheit, dient statt einer Vorrede, und bestimmt das Publikum so ziemlich, für welches dies seltsame Werk seyn kann." For the complete review see Stefan Kunze, *Beethoven: Die Werke im Spiegel seiner Zeit* (Laaber: Laaber-Verlag, 1987), 43; the translation in the text largely follows that in Sieghard Brandenburg, "Violin Sonatas, Cello Sonatas, and Variations," in *Ludwig van Beethoven,* ed. Joseph Schmidt-Görg and Hans Schmidt (New York: Praeger, 1970), 140.

3. For information on this performance, see Alexander Thayer, *Thayer's Life of Beethoven,* rev. and ed. Elliot Forbes (Princeton, N.J.: Princeton University Press, 1967), 332, citing Franz Gerhard Wegeler and Ferdinand Ries, *Biographische Notizen über Beethoven* (Coblenz, 1838), 82–83. For more on Bridgetower, see F. G. Edwards, "George P. Bridgetower and the Kreutzer Sonata," *Musical Times* 49 (1908): 302.

4. These ideas were first presented at the meeting of the American Musicological Society in Montréal, Canada, in November 1993; see Suhnne Ahn, "The French Connection: Kreutzer's Grande Sonata," in "Genre, Style, and Compositional Procedure in Beethoven's 'Kreutzer' Sonata, Opus 47" (Ph.D. diss., Harvard University, 1997), 137–94.

5. Wegeler and Ries, *Biographische Notizen,* 83.

6. Douglas Johnson, Alan Tyson, and Robert Winter, *The Beethoven Sketchbooks: History, Reconstruction, Inventory,* (Berkeley: University of California Press, 1985), 124–36.

7. Sieghard Brandenburg, "Zur Textgeschichte von Beethovens Violinsonate, op. 47," *Musik, Edition, Interpretation: Gedenkschrift Gunther Henle,* ed. Martin Bente (Munich: Henle, 1980), 111–24.

8. See Ahn, "Genre," 198–200.

9. Hans Schmidt, "Die Beethovenhandschriften des Beethovenhauses in Bonn," *Beethoven Jahrbuch VII, Jahrgang 1969/1970* (Bonn: Beethovenhaus, 1971), 229–30.

10. See Frank Peters, "The Phantom Supercollector of Buried Treasures," *St. Louis Post-Dispatch,* 21 January 1973, p. 5C.

11. For analysis see Christopher Reynolds, "Ends and Means in the Second Finale to Beethoven's Op. 30, no. 1," *Beethoven Essays: Studies in Honor of Elliot Forbes,* ed. Lewis Lockwood and Phyllis Benjamin (Cambridge, Mass.: Harvard University Dept. of Music, 1984), 127–45.

12. See Lewis Lockwood, "Earliest Sketches for the Eroica Symphony," *Beethoven: Studies in the Creative Process* (Cambridge, Mass.: Harvard University Press, 1992), 134–50.

13. For a discussion of this aspect of the work, see Ahn, "Genre," 12–15, 28–30, 242–44.

14. See ibid., 203–16.

15. Heinrich Christoph Koch, *Musikalisches Lexicon* (Frankfurt, 1802; repr., Hildesheim: G. Olms, 1964), cols. 355–56 (my translation).

16. William Newman, "Concerning the Accompanied Clavier Sonata," *Musical Quarterly* 33 (1947): 327–49.

17. Ibid., 330–31. Newman echos this statement in a discussion of Mozart's sonatas: "The growing independence of the Mozart violin part, from an optional, truly dispensable ad-

junct to a full *concertante* partner, makes a fascinating, significant story in itself" (*The Sonata in the Classic Era* [New York: Norton, 1983], 491). Newman's use of the term *concertante* is curiously casual, for the meaning of the term is not immediately evident. Mozart did not use the term to describe his own sonatas. As will be shown, Newman's description of concertante in Mozart's sonatas seems to be applied retrospectively.

18. Max Rostal's *Beethoven, the Sonatas for Piano and Violin: Thoughts on Their Interpretation* (London: Toccata, 1985), 131–61, provides performance suggestions for both pianist and violinist. Rostal proceeds throughout the piece phrase by phrase, emphasizing the difficulty of specific passages. In addition, the first review of Opus 47 in the *Allgemeine Musikalische Zeitung,* 28 August 1805, cols. 769–72, underscores the difficulty of the work in the following passage: "If two virtuosi to whom nothing remains difficult, who possess so much spirit and understanding that, with practice, they could write similar works themselves, and who are so engrossed in the spirit of the work as a whole that they are not disturbed by the most peculiar excrescences in detail;—if such virtuosi get together, rehearse the work (because even they must do this), wait for the right moment when people can and will enjoy even the most grotesque things provided that they are done with spirit, and play it at that moment—then they will derive full, rich enjoyment from it" (in Brandenburg, "Violin Sonatas," 140–41).

19. See Owen Jander, "The Kreutzer Sonata as Dialogue," *Early Music* 16 (1988): 34–49. A detailed discussion of his arguments is contained in Ahn, "Genre," 203–16.

20. See Claude Palisca, ed., *Norton Anthology of Western Music,* 2 vols. (New York: Norton, 1980), 2:124–55.

21. Martin Staehelin used the lack of repeated thematic material in the solo instruments as a criterion for determining the inauthenticity of one of Mozart's concertante. Staehelin initially excluded the sinfonia concertante labeled KV. Anh. I/9 (279b) from Mozart's oeuvre because a manuscript copy contains numerous thematic repetitions, a trait *not* found in the works by Mozart. In reconstructing the work, however, Levin overturns Staehelin's conclusions. According to Levin, thematic repetitions are present because of the history of the extant sources—manuscript but not autograph copies. Preserving the lack of literal repetition as a criterion, Levin nevertheless restores the sinfonia concertante to Mozart's output.

Although the notion of absence of literal repetition was first raised in discussions of Mozart, it is especially interesting that the same feature is apparent in Opus 47. More specifically, Beethoven's treatment of thematic and melodic material between the two instruments eschews literal repetition. For a full discussion see Robert Levin, *Who Wrote the Mozart Four-Wind Concertante?* (Stuyvesant, N.Y.: Pendragon, 1988), 83.

22. Recall the famous account of the first performance of this work preserved in Thayer, *Thayer's Life,* 333. During the first performance Bridgetower displayed a gesture of spontaneity by playing an arpeggio comparable to the piano's during the repeat of the exposition at measure 36. According to the account, Beethoven jumped up and said: "Noch einmal, mein lieber Bursch [once more, my dear boy]!"

23. The comparison of measure 153 and measure 165 with measure 474 and measure 486, respectively, raises an old question. In the exposition, a G♯ rather than a G♮ is written on the third beat of measure 165, creating a cross-relation with the harmony within the measure and also with the harmony in the previous measure. Some editions, such as the International Edition, omit the G♯ on the basis of the dissonant cross-relation created, although the sketches in the Wielhorsky sketchbook and the preliminary autograph confirm that Beethoven intended the G♯. Nonetheless, since the passage "sounds strange" with the G♯, Brandenburg, the editor of the violin sonatas, took the trouble to note that the sharp is "in the original edition." The question remains, then: why does the recapitulation in the comparable passage contain a C♮ and not a C♯? One reason is that the engraver's copy, which Simrock used for the first edition, contains a C♮ rather than a C♯. Clearly Brandenburg took

this as evidence when deciding to retain the C♯ in the recapitulation. The engraver's copy is a compilation of several copyists, however, and the missing autograph of the work, should it resurface, may help in solving this question. For a summary of the G♯ dilemma in the first movement, see Boris Schwarz, review of *Kniga eskizov Beethoven za 1802–1803 gody,* by Natan Fishman, in *Musical Quarterly* 47 (1963): 525.

24. Boris Schwarz, "Beethoven and the French Violin School," *Musical Quarterly* 44 (1958): 431–47.

25. Schmidt, "Beethovenhandschriften des Beethovenhauses," 636, item 637. See also Richard Kramer, "On the Dating of Two Aspects in Beethoven's Notation for Piano," in *Beethoven-Kolloquium 1977,* ed. Rudolf Klein (Kassel: Bärenreiter, 1978), 160–73. In the latter Kramer discusses the expansion of the piano range present on the leaves that belong to the Wielhorsky sketchbook. For more on the sources to Opus 37, see Hans-Werner Küthen, *Kritische Bericht,* pt. 3, vol. 2, for the Klavierkonzert No. 3 in C minor, Opus 37, *Beethoven Werke* (Munich: Henle, 1984). For Plantinga's discussion of the dating of Opus 37, see Leon Plantinga, "When Did Beethoven Compose His Third Piano Concerto?" *Journal of Musicology* 7 (1989): 275–307; and idem, *Beethoven's Concertos* (New York: Norton, 1999), 113–35.

26. William Drabkin, "Towards the 'Symphonic Concerto' of the Middle Period: Beethoven's Third and Fourth Piano Concertos," in *Ludwig van Beethoven: Atti del Convegno Internationale di Studi,* ed. Giuseppe Pugliese (Treviso: Matteo editore, 1988), 93–103. See also Donald Tovey, *Concertos and Choral Works* (Oxford: Oxford University Press, 1989), 69–84.

27. Ibid.

28. Michael Thomas Roeder, *A History of the Concerto* (Portland, Ore.: Amadeus, 1994), 185. Charles Rosen (*The Classical Style: Haydn, Mozart, Beethoven* [New York: Viking, 1971], 389–90) also devotes attention to the uniqueness of the opening of Opus 58. Rosen, however, attempts to draw a larger continuous tradition between Beethoven and Mozart, especially the similarity between the openings of Beethoven's Opus 58 and Mozart's K. 271. He writes: "Most important of all, Beethoven takes up the conception of the dramatic entrances of the soloist where Mozart had left it, and so realizes some of his own most imaginative ideas. Two of the most original effects in the Fourth Concerto are paradoxically occasions for the only direct references in the work to Mozart. The entrance of the first measure of the work immediately brings to mind the opening of K. 271, where Mozart has the piano enter in the second measure in direct answer to the opening orchestral motif. Beethoven's opening, at once poetically resonant and reticent, recalls Mozart's only conceptually, but they both result from a similar logic or way of thought."

29. See Rosen, *The Classical Style,* 333. In addition, I would like to thank Harry Ballan and Robert Kapilow for their informal yet stimulating discussions on the rise of the individual and its relevance to change in the nineteenth-century concerto. These ideas were exchanged in a seminar on Mozart's works held at Yale University during the fall of 1985.

5. THE INTRODUCTION TO BEETHOVEN'S "KREUTZER" SONATA: A HISTORICAL PERSPECTIVE

William Drabkin

Early in 1803 Beethoven, supposedly on the threshold of a new creative phase, composed two movements for violin and piano—a sonata form and a set of variations—that he put together with a previously composed finale to make up a sonata in the key of A. This sonata, called the "Kreutzer" after the illustrious violinist to whom the first edition was dedicated, has been popular in the concert hall ever since its first performance by Beethoven and George Bridgetower on 24 May 1803. The work's chief appeal lies in the technical challenges it offers to the performers, which were unprecedented in the sonata literature at the time of its composition; its musical content, however, has not attracted a great deal of interest from Beethoven scholars and music theorists (exceptions will be noted later). In this respect it is typical of classical violin music in general, which attracts a large public following yet does not enjoy a commensurate place in musicological and theoretical forums.

Nonetheless, the slow introduction to the first movement is sometimes singled out for its remarkable harmonic organization, in which the usual progression from minor to major—from "darkness" to "light"—is strikingly reversed. Donald Tovey had no doubts about the importance of the "Kreutzer" in this respect, calling the introduction to the first movement "one of the landmarks in musical history." This statement appears in one of his short articles on chamber music, published posthumously in a supplementary volume to his *Essays in Musical Analysis.* Dating from the time of Tovey's activities as a concert organizer and artist at St. James's Hall, London, at the turn of the century, it may reflect the generosity of spirit he characteristically displayed toward all the music he performed. Whether or not he overstated the case for the seminal status of the work, he mentioned only two "sources" for its construction and was silent about its possible influence on nineteenth-century instrumental music.[1]

Example 5.1 provides a score of the Adagio sostenuto. The antecedent phrase (mm. 1–4), for solo violin, is purely and simply in A major; this is what determines the initial key signature of three sharps. The consequent phrase, for solo piano, likewise begins on an A major chord, but the content of the next two bars makes us hear it as a secondary dominant—V/IV—in A minor. The world of major has now been left behind, but the alternative, parallel key proves to be of only limited service in the consequent phrase, which Beethoven has designed to be congruent to measures 1–4.

The crux comes when measure 3 is mapped onto measure 7 in the consequent. The double-stop c♯¹–a¹ becomes an F-major chord; the effect of this chord, the submediant of A minor, is surprising, but it is still a plausible response from the full-voiced piano to the thinner texture of the solo violin, as the double-stop can be read not only as a tonic without its fifth but also as a submediant without its root. The big B-minor chord, on the other hand, cannot automatically be translated into A minor, since the II in major does not have a stable equivalent in minor; in reconfiguring the harmony, as illustrated in example 5.2, Beethoven preserves a sense of parallelism by using D minor—IV in A minor—as a substitute for the II. Crucially, however, he allows F to remain in the bass, allowing the D-minor chord to fall more naturally into place as a II⁶ of C major, the relative key. This harmonic pivoting is assisted by the chromatic progression in the bass, F–F♯–G.

The interplay of piano and violin momentarily confirms these intentions, but the ensuing sequence eventually swings the tonality once more back toward A minor. The chromatic progression reappears at measure 12, but this time it is halted at the next downbeat on the G-major chord without being allowed to spill over onto the expected C major. Now Beethoven begins gradually to dismantle the forces that had been working for C major. The embellishing diminished chord already contains the seed of destruction, the note B♭, which softens the blow when G major—still a possible dominant of C in measure 14—turns to minor and thus finally loses its potential as a dominant chord (see example 5.3). With a return to C major now ruled out, Beethoven continues the process of chromatic substitution, removing the F♯ that had allowed D to function as a dominant for three bars and replacing it with F♮. From here it is but a small step to regain the piano chords from measures 5–6 that had once forecast A minor so decisively.

So the introduction ends in A minor, and the following Presto is also in A minor; the sonata remains in the orbit of that key throughout the Andante con variazioni, in F major—the normal submediant of the home key and a conventional choice for the middle movement of a sonata. At the start of the final Presto, however, Beethoven turns back to A major and remains there until the piece ends. As is well known, the *fortissimo* A-major chord was prefixed to this movement at a late stage, helping to sweep away the residues of A minor and F major.[2]

EXAMPLE 5.1. Beethoven, Violin Sonata in A Major, Opus 47, first movement, mm. 1–21

EXAMPLE 5.2. Opus 47, first movement, derivation of harmony of mm. 5–9 from mm. 1–4

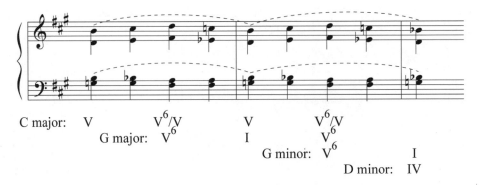

EXAMPLE 5.3. Opus 47, first movement, harmonic analysis of mm. 13–15

The first issue that interests me here is the extent to which the tonal plan of the "Kreutzer" is new. Was it unprecedented for a sonata movement to begin in a major key, only to end up in the minor? The opposite procedure is far more common: sonata forms in major are often preceded by introductions, or introductory gestures, that are set in or suggest the parallel minor. Works such as Mozart's "Dissonant" Quartet, Haydn's last two London symphonies, and Beethoven's own Fourth Symphony and third of the "Razumovsky" Quartets are a few examples that immediately come to mind. A number of chamber works by Haydn and Mozart are concerned with the relationship of minor to major, and Beethoven apparently knew some of these quite well; might he have relied on any of these as models for the "Kreutzer"? And what of its clear ending in major: is this simply a *tierce de Picardie* writ large, or is there a connection to the work's opening bars?

Let me start by offering a provisional answer to the last of these questions. The sonata's overall shape—two movements based on a reference point of A minor, with a finale in major—recalls the plan of two chamber works by Mozart. One of these, the String Quintet K. 516, Beethoven certainly came to know at some point in his life, for he noted its main theme in one of his conversation books.[3] As table 5.1 shows, the plan of this work closely resembles that of the "Kreutzer." Its first two movements are in G minor; it has a slow movement in the submediant, E♭ major; and following a suspenseful introduction, it concludes with a cheerful Rondo in G major. The Piano Quartet K. 478, another work that Beethoven is likely to have known,[4] resembles the "Kreutzer" more closely in that it behaves as a typical piece in minor for two movements but shifts abruptly to the tonic major, without any transition to bridge the work's serious beginning and joyful conclusion.

Table 5.1. Tonal Plans of the "Kreutzer" Sonata and Two Chamber Works by Mozart

Beethoven, Sonata for Violin and Piano, Opus 47			
	Adagio sostenuto–Presto	Andante	Presto
	A major–A minor		F major A major
A minor: $I^{\sharp 3}$–I		VI	$I^{\sharp 3}$
Mozart, String Quintet in G Minor, K. 516			
	Allegro MINUETTO: Allegretto	Adagio ma non troppo	Adagio–Allegro
	G minor G minor (trio in major)	E♭ major	G minor–G major
G minor: I $I(-I^{\sharp 3}-I)$		VI	$I-I^{\sharp 3}$
Mozart, Piano Quartet in G minor, K. 478			
	Allegro	Andante	RONDO: Allegro moderato
	G minor	B♭ major	G major
G minor: I		III	$I^{\sharp 3}$

In addition, a small group of Haydn's string quartets from the mid-1790s turn from major to minor before ending in the major, although the proportions are different from those of the "Kreutzer" Sonata. In two of these, Opus 76, Nos. 1 and 3, Haydn stretches the tension of the home key over the full reach of the quartet by denying listeners the light-hearted finale they would rightly expect: as can be seen in table 5.2, the last movement is set in minor up to and including the reprise of the principal theme.

Of course, these examples occur in pieces in which the major mode has already been established beyond doubt: the "happy ending" does not come as a surprise but is merely delayed by a few minutes. There are, however, pieces in which things start to go wrong sooner, so to speak. A work frequently invoked in discussions of the "Kreutzer" is Mozart's K. 379, an earlier sonata for violin and piano in which an Adagio in major prepares an Allegro in minor (see table 5.3). Nevertheless, to call the Adagio of K. 379 a slow introduction, as the literature sometimes does (and as the bar numbering in the *Neue Mozart-Ausgabe* implies it to be), is misleading, since it behaves in many respects like the first movement of the sonata, with a sonata-form exposition (repeated) followed by a substantial development and a retransition to the tonic.[5] Only the recapitulation is missing: the retransition turns abruptly away from the major five bars before the double bar, launching the Allegro in G minor. (The piece ends with a theme and variations in which G major is restored.) A similar plan is found in the Andante and Fugue, for violin and piano, K. 402 (also outlined in table 5.3), which is probably a sonata fragment: a sonata-form exposition and development in A major are used to prepare a fast movement in A minor. (This time the bar numbering, in the same volume of the *Neue Mozart-Ausgabe,* suggests two separate movements.)[6]

Together with a number of other Mozart violin sonatas published in the 1780s and 1790s, the G-major K. 379 was apparently well known to Beethoven: his early Piano Quartet in E♭, WoO 36, No. 1, written at the age of fourteen, follows its plan of movements and keys, and its opening Adagio assai bears a distinct thematic similarity to its model (examples 5.4–5.7). Note especially the rhythmic profile of the two hymnlike opening themes and the continuation in faster note values (beginning at m. 12 in Mozart and at m. 8 in Beethoven).

Sharper turns from major to minor crop up in a number of slow introductions in the Viennese symphony of the 1780s and 1790s, beginning with Mozart's Symphony in D Major, K. 504, of 1786. The "Prague" Symphony has a much more extensive introduction than does the "Kreutzer" Sonata: not only is it twice as long, but it is based on a contrasting group of thematic ideas rather than a single theme. True, the seeds of change are sown as early as the fourth bar, in which the unprepared A♯ in the bass anticipates the B♭ in the third bar of the minor section (example 5.8), but the effect of the sudden D-minor *forte* in measure 16 is unsettling, almost frightening. The introduction to the "Prague" has already been linked to another work generally regarded as transitional in Beethoven's creative development: this is the Second Symphony, which was composed in 1801–2 and shares

Table 5.2. Tonal Plans of Two String Quartets from Haydn's Opus 76

No. 1 in G major

	Allegro con spirito	Adagio sostenuto	MENUETTO: Presto	Allegro ma non troppo					
				exposition		development		recapitulation	
				m. 1	25	73		122	139
	G major	C major	G major	G min	B♭	B♭ min		G minor	G maj
G major:	I	IV	I	$I^{\flat3}$ …				… $I^{\flat3}$	

No. 3 in C major ("Emperor")

	Allegro	Poco adagio	MENUETTO: Allegro	FINALE: Presto					
				exposition		development		recapitulation	
				m. 1	21	73		119	152
	C major	G major	C major	C min …	E♭	E♭ …		C min	C maj
C major:	I	V	I	$I^{\flat3}$ …				… $I^{\flat3}$	

Table 5.3. Tonal Plans of Two Mozart Violin Sonatas and an Early Beethoven Piano Quartet

Mozart, K. 379

	Adagio	Allegro	THEMA: Andantino cantabile
	G major	G minor	G major
G major:	I (ending on V of $I^{\flat 3}$)	$I^{\flat 3}$	I

Mozart, K. 402 (Andante and Fugue, incomplete)

	Andante, ma un poco adagio	Allegro moderato	
	A major	A minor	
A major:	I (ending on V of $I^{\flat 3}$)	$I^{\flat 3}$	

Beethoven, WoO 36, No. 1

	Adagio assai	Allegro con spirito	THEMA: Cantabile
	E♭ major (incomplete)	E♭ minor	E♭ major
E♭ major:	I (ending on V of $I^{\flat 3}$)	$I^{\flat 3}$	I

EXAMPLE 5.4. Mozart, Violin Sonata in G Major, K. 379, first movement, mm. 1–14

EXAMPLE 5.5. Beethoven, Piano Quartet in E♭ Major, WoO 36, No. 1, first movement, mm. 1–10

EXAMPLE 5.6. Mozart, K. 379, first movement, mm. 44–49, and second movement, mm. 1-6

EXAMPLE 5.7. Beethoven, WoO 36, no.1, first movement, mm. 63–69, and second movement, mm. 1–9

EXAMPLE 5.7. Cont.

its key and first-movement format with the "Prague." And although the confrontation between major and minor in its opening Adagio is not quite so distinctly profiled, the contrast between sharp and flat keys is reinforced by the closer juxtaposition of A♯ and B♭ in the bass early in the movement (see example 5.9).

The "Prague" was quickly followed by a series of symphonies by Haydn in which the relationship of major to minor becomes a prominent compositional feature within the slow introduction or between the introduction and the following Allegro. The opening Adagio of Symphony No. 92 (1788) and all the slow introductions to the "London" symphonies (1791–95) develop this idea—each in a different way—and most of these symphonies shift distinctly from major to minor, or turn toward the flat end of the tonal spectrum, about halfway through the introduction (see table 5.4).

Of all these works, Symphony No. 96, in D major, composed in 1791, most closely anticipates the "Kreutzer" (example 5.10). The first six bars of the Adagio are straightforwardly in D major. Then the music begins again, this time with F♮ as the third note of the broken chord. (Characteristically, Haydn saves the defining

EXAMPLE 5.8. Mozart, Symphony in D Major, K. 504, first movement, mm. 1–4 and mm. 16–19

EXAMPLE 5.9. Beethoven, Second Symphony in D Major, Opus 36, first movement, mm. 8–12

Table 5.4. Tonal Plans of the Slow Introductions to Eight of Haydn's "London" Symphonies

Symphony	Key	Slow Introduction
No. 92	G	Bars 1–10 firmly in tonic major; bar 11 introduces the minor third as a chromatic passing tone; the final phrase dwells on an augmented sixth chord, further hinting at minor
No. 93	D	Bars 1–10 firmly in tonic major; the Neapolitan sixth chord in bar 11 leads to the dominant colored by the tonic minor
No. 94	G	Bars 1–8 firmly in tonic major; C major in bar 9 interpreted as the V of F minor (♮VII♭3), leading to the dominant colored by the tonic minor
No. 96	D	Bars 1–6: antecedent phrase in major; bars 7ff.; consequent in minor
No. 99	E♭	Flat sixth (C♭) in bars 9–10 reinterpreted as leading note to C minor; introduction ends on the V of C minor
No. 100	G	Bars 1–13 establish G major; G-minor theme enters abruptly in bar 14; introduction ends on the V of G minor
No. 102	B♭	Bars 1–10 establish tonic major; bar 11 introduces the minor third leading to the dominant colored by minor
No. 103	E♭	Bars 1–13 establish tonic major, and bars 14–25 confirm it; F-minor chord in bar 29 reinterpreted as the IV of C minor; introduction ends on the V of C minor.

EXAMPLE 5.10. Haydn, Symphony No. 96 in D major, first movement, mm. 1–21

EXAMPLE 5.10. Cont.

feature of the triad, the minor third, until the last possible moment.) The rest of introduction—right up to the oboe solo in measures 15–17—remains poised on the dominant of D minor, and the tension is broken only by the return of F♯ at the start of the Allegro.

Despite the similarity of design, the "Kreutzer" sets minor against major in a different way. Rather than introduce the tonic minor as an alternative outcome of the dominant chord, Beethoven actually modulates away from A major early on, establishing a position from which a sonata-allegro in A minor is the only sensible outcome. The move to C major in measures 7–9 is thus of critical importance. Nowhere in the other slow introductions under consideration—in Symphony No. 96, Haydn's other London symphonies, Mozart's K. 504, and Beethoven's Second Symphony—is there a comparable move to the mediant, which will actually confirm the minor key as a tonal center independent of the parallel major.[7]

While I am therefore inclined to reject the direct influence of either Mozart or Haydn, whose moves from major to minor must be understood more as digressions than modulations, it is possible to see the "Kreutzer" introduction as the result of Beethoven's honing the idea of a major-to-minor beginning to a minimum of musical material. The early piano quartet, in juxtaposing movements in

E♭ major and E♭ minor, follows its Mozart model quite closely—slavishly, one might say. The Second Symphony, taking its cue from Mozart's "Prague," compresses these contrasts inside a single section. The "Kreutzer," written in the following year, sets minor against major within a single period and then breaks free of eighteenth-century models altogether by developing toward a sonata-allegro movement in minor.

One is tempted to take this interpretation a stage further by relating the key of the "Kreutzer" finale, which already existed when Beethoven set about composing a new violin sonata in 1803, to the A-major beginning of the opening Adagio sostenuto. That is, he would not have been content to write a piece that merely ended brilliantly in a major key without in some way anticipating that ending; in this respect the plan of the "Kreutzer" represents an advance—in Beethovenian terms—over that of Mozart's G-minor chamber pieces. The first sketch for the slow introduction, on page 167 of the Wielhorsky sketchbook, is marked "Introduzione" and shows a series of violin double-stops in 3/4 time, but the implied harmony is A minor. In the subsequent pages, however, the entries for the introduction consistently support an implied key signature of three sharps.[8] This does not mean that Beethoven would have found an A-minor beginning (i.e., a first movement entirely based around A minor) unacceptable per se, yet once he hit on the possibility of beginning in A major, he did not waver from this idea.

Of course, the plan to move from the minor toward a strong ending in major is something that Beethoven was to work out in a number of interesting ways, from the Cello Sonata in G Minor, with its unaffected shift at the end of the first of its two movements (the process is repeated in the last piano sonata, composed a quarter-century later), to the triumphant Fifth and Ninth Symphonies. That is not, however, to deny the "Kreutzer," together with its eighteenth-century antecedents, a role in developing this idea.

Having offered a perspective on the origins of the "Kreutzer" introduction, I now turn to its possible influence on later composers by examining two nineteenth-century chamber works in which the relationship of major to minor—in both cases, of A major to A minor—is a crucial feature.

Mendelssohn's String Quartet, Opus 13, the first of his six works in the genre, is generally viewed as an early—and precocious—response to Beethoven's late style. Dating from the summer and autumn of 1827, a few months after Beethoven's death, it is replete with reminiscences of Beethoven's String Quartet, Opus 132, also in A minor, and other quartets, but its slow movement contains an unmistakable reference to Mozart's String Quintet in G Minor, which is further evidence of that work's early canonical status.[9]

Table 5.5 shows that the whole piece is held in the orbit of A minor, except for the very beginning and very end, which are in A major. The piece actually enjoys

Table 5.5. Tonal Plan of Mendelssohn's String Quartet, Opus 13

	Adagio–Allegro vivace A major–A minor A minor	Adagio non lento F major	INTERMEZZO A minor	Presto A minor	–Adagio come I A major
A minor:	I♯3–I	VI	I	I	– I♯3

a musicological double identity: some writers call it a quartet in A *minor;* others, a quartet in A *major.*[10]

Was the "Kreutzer" introduction a possible inspiration for Mendelssohn? In the quartet the Adagio sets a scene of peaceful contemplation by invoking the song "Frage" (which was published alongside it in 1830, as well as appearing in Mendelssohn's second collection of lieder, Opus 9). That is, Mendelssohn uses a "'song with words' without words," so to speak, from which arises a tempestuous string quartet whose outer movements are set in unrelieved minor. One cannot ignore the possibility of a theatrical gesture here—the musical equivalent to a play within a play—or of a programmatic interpretation: to the first line of the song, which asks, "Ist es wahr?" (is it true?), the quartet may be thought to reply, "Nein, es ist nicht wahr!" (no, it's not true).[11] Not only is the opposition of mood between the quartet and its framing music about as stark as one could imagine, but this quality is accentuated by the choice of E minor as the secondary key of both outer movements and, in the finale, by the domination of the central section by a recall of the slow-movement fugato.

Compared to the "Kreutzer," the conflict between major and minor is played out on a different level over the quartet as a whole, not merely within the introduction. Nevertheless, the design of Mendelssohn's Adagio, in terms of phrase structure and general contour, is not so different from that of Beethoven's Adagio sostenuto. Example 5.11 reproduces the first of the two A-major sections that frame the quartet. Mendelssohn's first four bars make a harmonically complete statement in A major. This phrase is now set in a higher octave, with a new, destabilizing harmony, and extended by a sequential passage that eventually restores A major. Admittedly, one cannot speak about a contrast of instrumentation or modal opposition, but the change of register (and dynamic) in measure 5 does suggest a new type of sonority, a different quartet timbre. In addition, the surprise F♯-major chord in measure 6, which also sets the sequence in motion, has an effect similar to the harmonic surprises in the consequent phrase of the "Kreutzer," that is, the D-minor chord in measure 5 and deceptive move to F major on the downbeat of measure 7.

The quartet differs from the sonata, however, in its obvious efforts to integrate a conventional multimovement plan into a unified conception by thematic and gestural links among and between its several movements.[12] These are more striking features, and my suggestion of a link between the two works is in no way intended to downgrade the well-documented kinship between late Beethoven and early Mendelssohn.

Allegro

EXAMPLE 5.11. Mendelssohn, String Quartet, Opus 13, first movement, beginning

My second example is a work from the end of the nineteenth century: Dvořák's Quintet for Piano and Strings, Opus 81, of 1887. As can be seen from table 5.6, the underlying modality of the quintet as a whole is A major, and in this respect the work does not bear comparison with either the "Kreutzer" Sonata or Mendelssohn's quartet. The opening gestures in the first movement not only oppose major and minor, however; they also bring to mind the associated relationship of introduction to continuation, for despite the continuity of tempo throughout the first movement, Dvořák deploys his themes and accompaniments in such a way as to give the illusion of slower introductory music giving way to a faster continuation.[13]

The Allegro ma non tanto begins as a cello solo with piano accompaniment; the eight-bar antecedent of the opening theme is restricted to the basic chords of A major (see example 5.12). In the consequent phrase, however, the leading note is lowered to G♮ and so converts the tonic chord to a V^7/IV. In this respect, Dvořák has taken the harmony one stage further than did Beethoven, who keeps the downbeat of measure 5 of the "Kreutzer" a simple A-major triad.

Dvořák's harmony continues to unfold more quickly. The resolution of the dominant seventh not only brings the flat third (in this respect following Beethoven) but intensifies the contrast of major and minor by introducing the flat sixth, B♭, above the bass D (see examples 5.13 and 5.14 for a comparison). In other words, where a single F♮ was enough for Beethoven to effect a surprise, Dvořák makes two changes to the antecedent chord in response to his explicit secondary dominant.

The major third in measure 14, at first seeming to countervail the thrust toward the minor, proves to be a chromatic passing tone, and the entry of the full quintet texture, with a new theme, confirms the arrival in A minor. This faster-sounding music will follow a standard path of ascending thirds, from the tonic to the mediant to the (major) dominant, much as Beethoven does in the Presto of the "Kreutzer." This is in itself not surprising, but instead of proceeding to a second group in the dominant, Dvořák works his way back to the beginning, as if to start the piece for a second time (m. 61). Now the first violin takes over from the solo cello: antecedent in A major (mm. 61–68); consequent in A minor (mm. 69–75); and new music in A minor, with triplet eighth notes conveying an even greater contrast of perceived tempo between the theme and its continuation (mm. 15ff.). The second attempt at a transition to a contrasting key area is more abrupt but

Table 5.6. Tonal Plan of Dvořák's Piano Quintet, Opus 81

	Allegro, ma non tanto A major	DUMKA F♯ minor	SCHERZO: Molto vivace A major	FINALE: Allegro A major
A major:	I	VI	I	I

EXAMPLE 5.12. Dvořák, Piano Quintet in A major, Opus 81, first movement, mm. 3–20

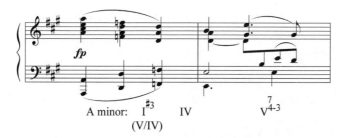

EXAMPLE 5.13. Harmonic analysis of Beethoven, Opus 47, first movement, mm. 5–6

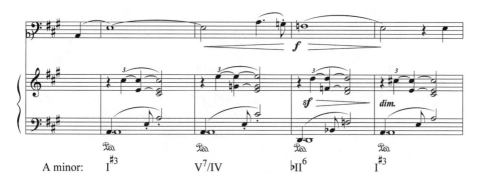

EXAMPLE 5.14. Dvořák, Opus 81, first movement, mm. 11–14

proves definitive. Having previously traversed the traditional path of I–III–V, Dvořák now avoids this typically classical option and instead turns to the mediant of A major.

The degree to which the first movement of the quintet is concerned with the contrast of major and minor may be judged by a survey of its thematic material. The principal themes in the movement, charted in figure 5.1, all give prominence to the descending tetrachord between the tonic, A, and the upper fifth, E, with the sixth and seventh degrees raised or lowered to distinguish the two modes. The technique of transforming major into minor by lowering the sixth and seventh degrees rather than the third is especially noticeable in the development, which is based mainly on the opening theme and consistently develops the minor version of its initial motive. The result is a piece that, although it is undisputedly in A major in terms of planning, places so much emphasis on thematic material and thematic development in minor keys that, as with the "Kreutzer," the overall mood of the piece is unfaithful to its governing key signature. The volte-face in the final pages provides an emphatic A-major ending (see example 5.15), yet one that is far from conclusive: the competition between the major and minor

FIGURE 5.1. First-movement themes in Dvořák's Opus 81, represented paradigmatically

EXAMPLE 5.15. Dvořák, Opus 81, first movement, ending

EXAMPLE 5.15. Cont.

tetrachords (compare mm. 397–99 with mm. 413–16) may remind us of the early conflict between major and minor, but it does not resolve it.

Without actually being unkind to the "Kreutzer," music critics have not been over-enthusiastic in praising its musical values. Walter Riezler's claim that it was in its time Beethoven's most important achievement in the field of sonata is probably beyond dispute,[14] but other writers, by judging the first movement to be the "finest," have relegated the work *as a whole* to something less than the status of a masterpiece. It is as if the end did not quite live up to the promise of the beginning.[15] The "Kreutzer" hardly ever figures in studies in music theory and analysis, in stark contrast to the surrounding sonatas for solo piano.[16] In Beethoven biographies it surfaces less as a transitional work between the first decade in Vienna and the so-called heroic phase than as an item of luggage in the composer's French travel kit, an accessory that he would find useful on an artistic trip to Paris that reportedly he intended to make around 1805.

It is also no exaggeration to say that the reception of the "Kreutzer" Sonata has had more to do with its name than with its musical content: between them, Leo Tolstoy and Leoš Janáček have immortalized the name of the piece without dwelling on the musical substance,[17] the sonata becoming more a vehicle for psychological interaction than an object of contemplation. Without denying the power of music (and human imagination) to leap across disciplinary boundaries, I hope to have demonstrated here that the intrinsically musical properties of the work also merit close examination and that perhaps they, too, have enjoyed a reception in the chamber music of composers who followed Beethoven.

Notes

1. Donald Francis Tovey, *Essays in Musical Analysis: Chamber Music,* ed. Hubert J. Foss (London: Oxford University Press, 1944), 135–36. Most of the essays are concerned with music for piano solo or with "chamber music"—as conventionally understood—with piano: piano quartets and quintets and accompanied sonatas.

2. See Sieghard Brandenburg, "Zur Textgeschichte von Beethovens Violinsonate Opus 47," in *Musik, Edition, Interpretation: Gedenkschrift Günther Henle,* ed. Martin Bente (Munich: Henle, 1980), 119–20. I am aware of only one earlier instance of a composer abruptly severing the tonal links between adjacent movements with a single chord: Haydn's String Quartet Opus 77, No. 2, in which a slow movement ending in D major, with F♯ in the melody, is followed by a finale in F major. How well Beethoven knew this piece, composed by his former teacher in 1799—that is, a few years before the "Kreutzer"—can only be guessed.

3. Beethoven, *Ludwig van Beethovens Konversationshefte,* vol. 10, ed. Dagmar Beck and Günther Brosche (Leipzig: Deutscher Verlag für Musik, 1993), 130. The passage, which dates from around 20 August 1826, was first discussed by Martin Staehelin in "Another Approach to Beethoven's Last String Quartet Oeuvre: The Unfinished String Quartet of 1826/27," in *The String Quartets of Haydn, Mozart, and Beethoven: Studies of the Autograph Manuscripts,* ed. Christoph Wolff (Cambridge, Mass.: Harvard University Dept. of Music, 1980), 313–15.

4. Lewis Lockwood has noted similarity with the "Spring" Sonata's finale; see this volume, p. 39 and example 2.16.

5. See Mozart, *Wolfgang Amadeus Mozart: Neue Ausgabe sämtliche Werke,* vol. 23, pt. 2, ed. Eduard Reeser (Kassel: Bärenreiter, 1965), 6: the first bar of the Allegro is numbered "50" and follows the opening forty-nine-bar Adagio.

6. Ibid., 176: the bar numbering of the Allegro moderato (the fugue) begins again from "1," following the seventy-five-bar Andante, ma un poco adagio. K. 402 is one of a number of pieces for violin and piano composed in 1782 but left unfinished. The fugue was itself unfinished and given by Mozart's widow to Maximilian Stadler to complete. It is impossible to tell how Mozart would have continued the piece, which was begun a year after the G-major sonata.

7. In this respect the "Kreutzer" marks a new direction in the structuring of slow introductions, which can also be heard as an opposition of B♭ minor and B minor in Symphony No. 4 and of A major and C major (later F major) in Symphony No. 7.

8. All known sketches for the first two movements of the "Kreutzer" are transcribed in Natan Fishman's edition of the Wielhorsky sketchbook: *Kniga eskizov Beethoven za 1802–1803 gody* 3 vols. (Moscow: Gos. Muzykal'noe izd-vo, 1962). Brandenburg improves the transcriptions of the first and sketches for the introduction ("Zur Textgeschichte," 113) and was the first to give a correct reading of Beethoven's word "introduzione." He was wrong to assert, however, that "all essential features of the completed work are shown in the very earliest phase of the work," since the key of the opening bars had not yet been fixed.

9. The Adagio non lento of Opus 13 is far more than a catalogue of Mendlessohn's favorite chamber music themes; nevertheless, there are clear references to the Cavatina of Opus 130 (compare the minor seventh chord in mm. 6–7, 16–17, etc., with Beethoven's mm. 8–9) and the fugato in the Allegretto ma non troppo of Opus 95 (compare Mendelssohn's m. 20 with Beethoven's m. 35). More striking still are measures 46–51, marked "poco più animato," which recycle the rhythms of the violin solo and syncopated accompaniments in the slow movement of Mozart's K. 516 (mm. 28–32).

Mendelssohn's early acquaintance with Beethoven's late quartets is documented by his April 1828 letter to the Swedish composer Adolf Fredrik Lindblad, written only months after the completion of Opus 13 and praising the Cavatina of Opus 130 for its special emotional qualities and all the quartets for their effective integration of disparate movements and sections into a aesthetically satisfying whole. The letter is partly transcribed in Wulf Kunold, *Felix Mendelssohn-Bartholdy und seine Zeit* (Laaber: Laaber-Verlag, 1984), 114.

10. Writers who have commented extensively on its relationship with Beethoven's Opus 132 invariably refer to it as an A-minor quartet: see John Horton, *Mendelssohn Chamber Music* (London: British Broadcasting Corporation, 1972); Friedhelm Krummacher, *Mendelssohn—der Komponist: Studien zur Kammermusik für Streicher* (Munich: Wilhelm Fink, 1978); and Kunold, *Felix Mendelssohn-Bartholdy.* Mendelssohn himself refers to his "A minor quartet" in a letter to his father, dated 31 March 1832 and quoted in Arnd Richter, *Mendelssohn: Leben, Werke, Dokumente* (Mainz: Piper/Schott, 1994).

By contrast, Opus 13 is deemed to be an A-major work in the Mendelssohn article in the *New Grove Dictionary of Music and Musicians,* ed. Stanley Sadie (London: Macmillan, 1980), and *Mendelssohn: Complete Chamber Music for Strings* (New York: Dover, 1978), a reprint of two volumes from the Mendelssohn collected edition of the 1870s.

11. Among the writers who have suggested a connection with the "question" in Beethoven's Opus 135 are Rudolf Stephan, who asks: "Ist aber die Frage jenes Liedes nicht mit der Frage Beethovens *Muß es sein?* nah verwandt [Is it not so that the question of that song is closely bound up with Beethoven's question, 'Must it be']?" See his essay "Über Mendelssohns Kontrapunkt: Vorläufige Bemerkungen," in *Das Problem Mendelssohn,* ed. Carl Dahlhaus (Regensburg: Gustav Bosse, 1974), 206.

Nonetheless, Eric Werner, for whom the song also has programmatic significance, believes that "the nucleus of *Ist es wahr?* occurs in Beethoven's sonata *Les Adieux,* itself a programmatic piece" (Werner, *Mendelssohn: A New Image of the Composer and His Age,* trans. Dika Newlin [New York: Free Press of Glencoe, 1963], 129).

12. Some of the more obvious features of this are the recurrence of the fugato from the Adagio non lento midway through the finale, the use of recitative to bridge the intermezzo and the finale, and the written-out trill between the notes E and F immediately before the main theme of the outer movements.

13. The only global marking implying an abrupt change of speed in the first movement is the "Tempo I" at the start of the recapitulation, but this follows a series of instructions to the pianist—tranquillo, sostenuto, largamente—that will inevitably result in a slowing down in the last twenty-three bars of the development section.

14. Walter Riezler, *Beethoven,* trans. G. D. H. Pidcock (London: Forrester, 1938), 132–33. In characterizing it as "the first truly great sonata," Riezler emphasizes that it is a work that has moved beyond the bounds of chamber music (i.e., the home) and that its true place is in the concert hall. This notion is repeated later, where the "Kreutzer" is grouped with the "Waldstein" and "Appassionata" as works that are more "spacious and magnificent" than the solo piano sonatas that preceded them yet written in a "simpler" manner (164).

15. For a dissenting view, see Owen Jander, "The 'Kreutzer' Sonata as Dialogue," *Early Music* 16 (1988): 34–49. This is an imaginative and wide-ranging discussion of the work, taking into account the rise of the "French Violin School" at the end of the century and the new, more brilliant styles of bowing that were developed around the turn of the century. I find it difficult, however, to accept two of the premises on which Jander's arguments depend: first, that Beethoven would have consulted a book on aesthetics for advice on ensuring unity in his musical compositions, and second, that the work's subtitle (as first published), "scritta in un stilo [*sic*] molto concertante, quasi come d'un concerto" (written in a marked concertante style, almost that of a concerto), has more to do with the partnership between the two instruments than with the brilliant style and bravura writing.

16. An exceptional case is the chapter entitled "The Thematic Pitch of the *Kreutzer* Sonata" in Rudolph Réti's posthumous *Thematic Patterns in Sonatas of Beethoven,* ed. Deryck Cooke (London: Faber and Faber, 1967), 145–65, an essay wholly devoted to processes of intervallic transformation in the music's thematic fabric.

17. Tolstoy's novella *The Kreutzer Sonata* (1890) was the inspiration for a piano trio by Janáček, which was first performed in 1909 and revised and rescored as a string quartet sixteen years later (the trio version does not survive). To be fair, the composer hints at the chorale-like second subject of Beethoven's first movement, for instance, in measures 15–19 of the third movement of the quartet, but this passage is part of a process of thematic development running throughout the movement.

6. THE VIOLIN SONATA IN G MAJOR, OPUS 96: PASTORAL, RHETORIC, STRUCTURE

Maynard Solomon

As a reminder of a harmonious world that once had flourished and that still persists in memory, pastoral style is classicism's primary image of simple contentment. But insofar as it is also the vehicle of love, loss, and longing, expressive of those things that remain forever beyond our grasp, it is central to the nostalgic concerns of romanticism. That is why poets and composers often have recourse to the pastoral genres as those best able to represent both classical serenity and romantic turbulence and to suggest ways in which these may be interrelated.

So, when a composer employs the language of pastoral it is not only to evoke picturesque scenes and legendary figures frozen in graceful and often vacuous poses, not only about lovelorn swains, the felicities of rustic life, the dignity of toil, the evidence of nature's bounty and profligacy, although it may often be about these as well, for, of course, these are crucial images of pastoral. Equally crucial, however, in the pastoral poetry of the ancient world—whether the Greek and Roman myths as set down by Ovid and Hesiod or the idylls and eclogues of Virgil, Theocritus, and Bion—is a sense that the idyllic state is a precarious one, vulnerable to being lost. From the start pastoral style has served as a global metaphor for an extensive range of affects and images, including burdensome issues and unsettling states of being. Oedipus himself started life as a pastoral hero, one of countless mythological highborn sons who were abandoned by their parents and secretly raised by shepherds or nurtured by gentle animals. Ancient pastoral poetry did not shrink from violence and death. Consider Bion's "Lament for Adonis": "Low on the hills is lying the lovely Adonis, and his thigh with the boar's tusk, his white thigh with the boar's tusk is wounded, and sorrow on Cypris he brings, as softly he breathes his life away. His dark blood drips down his skin of snow, beneath his brows his eyes wax heavy and dim, and the rose flees from his lip, and thereon the very kiss is dying, the kiss that Cypris will never forego."[1]

As a set of musical tropes pastoral mirrors an unbounded universe, and it provides copious means of sounding the main themes of a deeply felt existence within that universe. In its serenades, with their simulated guitar or lute accompaniments, it is the genre of love and, by extension, of every form of longing; in its echoes of forest murmurs and its evocation of pleasant landscapes, it is the image of solitary contentment and silent worship; as a mode of celebration of the ritual occasions of life, it is a music that magnifies the individual and the community and their reciprocal sense of shared traditions. Through its repertory of traditional dances it tells not only of love and courtship but of the body, the self, of abstract motion and the infinite degrees of velocity. Encoded in those dances—as Wye J. Allanbrook has shown—is data about distinctions of rank and divisions of class as well, but pastoral tends to alleviate such differences, bridging lower and higher, firstness and lastness.[2] In the elegiac mode of its andantes and adagios it has to do with loss, mourning, homage, and consolation. Its scherzos often unfold within a satiric or dithyrambic dimension: they enter a festive world, heralding resurrections. And its rondo-finales deliver on implied promises, illustrating the varieties of halcyon finality.

Pastoral is surely the quintessential style for chronicling scenarios of an initial state of harmony, its subsequent rupture, the yearning for its restoration, and of that restoration itself, transformed by the intervening experiences. That is why, in an era that prized classical texts and images, the deployment of pastoral mode was very often understood as an elaboration of the lineaments of a lost Arcadia, which, of all the imaginings of a paradisiac realm, was the utopian space perhaps most favored by refined sensibilities in the age of Mozart and Beethoven, a realm endlessly explorable, filled with activity and motion, while simultaneously gratifying sensuous and aesthetic longings for tranquility and beauty.

Arcadian imagery is thus a potent metaphor for a life that is fully experienced up to the moment of its extinction—and beyond, in historical memory. In the Arcadian mode we are at one with nature in all the turnings of its seasons and days, from spring to autumn, summer to winter, morning to evening, noon to midnight. Inevitably, then, Arcadia knows melancholy as well as joy, division as well as harmony, final sleep as well as first awakening.

Over the course of time, pastoral imagery in music increasingly focused on representations of idyllic existence, lives lived in nature's open realms, and uncomplicated amorousness. Pastoral style tended to become an unproblematic, conventional set of procedures appropriate to music imitative of the sounds of nature and picturing the supposed pleasures of rural life. At the extreme, pastoral's archaic power to disturb was set aside in favor of a burlesque commentary on rural life, featuring cheerful and picturesque subjects—say, Leopold Mozart's "Peasant Wedding," "Sleigh Ride," and "Sinfonia burlesca" or the boy Mozart's own pastoral quodlibet, "Gallimathias Musicum"—and utilizing naturalistic, imitative techniques that project a kind of lighthearted rustic stance. In pastoral music of the eighteenth century the disruption of an idyll is often represented merely as a misunderstanding between lovers or the arrival of bad weather—tempests, storms, lightning and thunder—soon followed by the return of calm. At the loftiest level of this process Haydn's oratorios *The Seasons* and *The Creation* are versions of a rational Enlightenment pastoral that locates harmonious patterns everywhere in a divine hierarchical arrangement of the universe.

In his Salzburg years Mozart developed a pastoral-style vocabulary to speak about love, beauty, nature, and connectedness. He used this language in the serenades, notturnos, and divertimentos that accompanied the ceremonies through which the community honored its leading citizens, celebrated its own achievements, and congratulated itself on its benevolence and wisdom, pretending—even believing—for a day that it had recovered the Golden Age of antiquity. Subsequently, except for a handful of Vienna-period serenades in which pastoral style predominates, Mozart used it in individual movements or extended sections of multimovement compositions as one so-called characteristic style among many— military, heroic, pathetic, serioso, learned, churchly—thereby heightening its dramatic effect but tending to narrow its range of potential representation. Thereby he crafted musical counterparts of idyllic or bucolic poetic interludes that the literary critic Renato Poggioli named "pastoral oases," where the poet evokes a secluded haven, secret garden, or other fleeting vision of an Arcadian haven within a nonpastoral universe: "Pastoral poetry makes more poignant and real the dream it wishes to convey when the retreat is not a lasting but a passing experience, acting as a pause in the process of living, as a breathing spell from the fever and anguish of being."[3]

Oases of this kind are frequently found in arias, serenades, romances, and rustic interludes of Mozart's operas. Allanbrook offers a profound pastoral reading of *Le nozze di Figaro,* seeing its pastoral as "a place out of time, where Eros presides." This, of course, is also the pastoral of Virgil and Watteau, but Allanbrook recognizes that pastoral is not bound by its mythological parameters and can take up residence in interior spaces as well. "The very unreality of Mozart's pastoral place," she writes, "is a guarantee of its possibility. It is merely a state of mind, called into being by a tacit understanding and defined by a nostalgic and otherworldly musical gesture."[4]

Beethoven initially took his cue from Mozart's later instrumental practice, however, and often reserved the pastoral style for minuet/scherzo or finale movements, the latter often cast in rondo form. A few examples of such finales include the "Pastoral" Sonata in D Major, Opus 28; the "Spring" Sonata in F Major for violin and piano, Opus 24; the first two piano concertos; and the Violin Concerto, Opus 61. In these works, as also in the opening scene of *Fidelio,* Beethoven uses pastoral style primarily to create a contrasting moment in a larger, nonpastoral design. Nostalgia and felicity are the main expressive features of such a moment, which in a single stroke can serve as a recognizable token of wistful longings or as shorthand for a state of well-being. The trio of a scherzo or minuet may evoke a pastoral setting—whether aristocratic, bucolic, mythological, or Edenic—that once was, that is well remembered, and that may come again. Pastoral finales are usually assured, hopeful, imbued with a confident expectation that the lost harmony between humanity and nature has been reestablished or, if not already present, is close at hand.

Pastoral is Beethoven's preferred voice only in his lieder, where it predominates, starting with such early Vienna songs as "Adelaide" and "Seufzer eines Ungeliebten" to the most characteristic songs of his maturity, including the Eight Songs, Opus 52; Six Songs, Opus 75; Three Goethe Lieder, Opus 83; and the valedictory "Abendlied unterm gestirnten Himmel," WoO 150, of 1820. The texts and musical gestures of his song cycle "An die ferne Geliebte" (1816) are replete with pastoral imagery, the whole indissolubly woven together as a symbol not only of the reunion of parted lovers but of their unity with nature and all nature's creatures.

Apart from his dances for the Redoutensaal and music for the ballet *The Creatures of Prometheus,* Opus 43, however, pastoral style is surprisingly sparse in Beethoven's early instrumental music. Evidently he had more momentous issues in mind—certainly the large-scale signature works of his "heroic" period were better suited to a more dynamic, heaven-storming rhetoric. Nevertheless, he sometimes set out to fuse pastoral and heroic styles as contending perspectives on the rupture in modern consciousness and as alternative ways of healing that rupture—either by recovering an Apollonian equanimity or by unloosing a Dionysian impulse. On one conspicuous occasion he showed a pastoral moment at the very instant of its fracture by disruptive forces. The two crashing chords that open the *Eroica* Symphony introduce a flowing pastoral negotiation of the common chord, a shepherd's yodel or an alphorn call that lasts less than two measures (it may be no accident that Mozart's *Bastien and Bastienne,* a pastoral singspiel derived from a text by Rousseau, opens with the same yodeling figure), until it is tipped into disequilibrium by a decisive descent through D to C♯ at measures 6–7. In a half-step Arcadia has been lost, thus launching a prolonged heroic narrative that will revert to the pastoral mode only in its contredanse finale.[5] But in two instrumental works written toward the close of the heroic period—and in "An die ferne Geliebte"— Beethoven deployed pastoral style throughout entire large-scale compositions instead of using individual pastoral topics as quick references to Arcadian states. The first of the instrumental works is the *Pastoral* Symphony, written in 1808; the second is his tenth and last violin sonata, the Sonata for Violin and Piano in G Major, Opus 96, written mainly in 1812–13.

The Sixth Symphony, of course, is replete with pastoral signifiers, including its main title, the famous programmatic movement descriptions, and a clutch of musical "topics"—homophonic style, drone basses, imitations of nature sounds, shepherd calls, folk instruments, and country dances—drawn from the roomy storehouse of such devices inventoried by eighteenth-century theorists and by scholars of our own time.[6] Beethoven, worried that he might have crossed the line into programmatic reductionism and perhaps hesitant to provide a target for snobbish critics, tried to reassure himself on this issue, writing on the sketches, "Pastoral Symphony—no [tone]painting, rather something in which the emotions that are aroused in people by the pleasures of the countryside are expressed, in which some of the feelings of country life are portrayed"; on the back of a first violin part he wrote the subtitle, "More the Expression of Feeling than Painting."[7] He eventually overcame his qualms and retained the descriptive titles in the *Pastoral* Symphony, but he followed his own advice to the letter in the Opus 96 sonata, which is devoid of literary allusions and permits listeners to find its pastoral signifiers for themselves.[8]

Each of the movements of the G-major sonata elaborates a distinctive version of pastoral, the whole constituting a series of sharply etched illustrations of the range and purposes of pastoral experience. The first movement, Allegro moderato, although untitled, is unabashedly an idyll, replete with bird calls, alpine horn arpeggios, drone basses, and figures that simulate the rustling, murmuring, and busy profusion of nature's sounds. The opening birdsong—resembling that of a skylark, noted for its song in upward flight—is a summons at daybreak, or an awakening of spring. A voice sounds, another responds, signaling that it is time to begin, for contact has been established. The heart also responds, overflows with joyful, confident, exultant feelings. The instrumental interplay is reminiscent of the conversational character of an eclogue: at the outset the violin and piano echo each other's motifs and then dovetail their efforts in long, soaring, arpeggiated lines in parallel motion (mm. 10–25) before embarking on another round of playful imitations, calls, and responses. Collaborating, the instruments genially traverse an agreed route: they are of one mind; neither needs to develop a separate perspective, let alone to advocate a contending view of experience. Instead, external concord finds inner confirmation, with each instrument completing, ratifying, and reinforcing the other (see example 6.1).

Several pastoral topics take turns displaying their wares: a D-major subsidiary theme in mock-processional style (mm. 41–58) laughingly skitters downward, landing in the center of a sequence of bagpipe drones at measures 58–59, which in turn gives way to an extended trill, crescendo, at measures 63–72. Those among Beethoven's contemporaries who viewed the world through lenses of alienation scenarios crafted by Rousseau and Schiller would have known that all this is too good to last. Melancholia and thoughts of loss and mortality must sooner or later break this spell. Indeed, we may even imagine that there is already a touch of mortality at the very opening, a latent *mal du pays* in the bird call itself. So it is no surprise when a melancholy strain makes its entrance, foreshadowed at measures 87 and 91–94, and then, in the development, expressed in a series of brooding

EXAMPLE 6.1. Beethoven, Violin Sonata in G Major, Opus 96, first movement, mm. 1–25

ostinatos on a sighing motif that dominate the texture until measures 116–26, when the instruments, no longer sighing in place or pressing to find an upward escape route, find relief in an echoing triplet figure that gracefully skims the depths of sadness (example 6.2).

Melancholic reflections give way to pizzicati and trills simulating more bird calls (mm. 139–41), but the G-major return to the opening lasts for only a moment before a shift into the parallel minor (mm. 148–49) transports the action to a mysterious landscape: the colors darken, and the movement drifts further into dream and dislocation. The twilight-hued G minor prepares the way for a transition into E♭ major (mm. 161–70), which looms large as a secondary key here and throughout the sonata. Seemingly, E♭ major has been designated as the key in which the idyll is yet to be regained, which is to say it appears to stand for a lost or misplaced aspect of Arcadia. In the course of the recapitulation and coda the melancholic strain is reactivated: the ostinato sighing motif returns for a full eight measures (mm. 230–38), issuing into a muted metamorphosis of the opening idyll. Despite the constantly renewed song of the lark, alone, in duet, or in an avian concert of cascading trills (mm. 262–67), and despite the insistently affirmative crescendo, ascending scale, and unequivocal cadence at the close, the ethereal modulations of the Allegro's last page continue to reverberate, even if they do not have the last word, bespeaking the precariousness of an ending which acknowledges that night must fall, even in Arcadia.

Whereas the Allegro moderato may bring to mind musical analogues of such venerable Arcadian poetic genres as the idyll or the eclogue, the slow movement,

EXAMPLE 6.2. Opus 96, first movement, mm. 116–22

Adagio espressivo, in E♭ major, speaks the eloquent language of pastoral's most plangent genre, the elegy. And just as G major has been firmly designated as expressive of idyllic states of being, both existent and recoverable, E♭ major is brought into play as a primary signifier of the elegiac mode, with its rhetoric of invocation, questioning, outcry, lament, consolation, and ultimate acceptance. Three themes create a tonal palette adequate to the scope and subtlety of the task. First, in legato phrases that move smoothly within the bar lines, without suspensions, and in four-part harmony appropriate to congregational music, the piano intones a symmetrical eight-measure hymn to make known the mournful nature of the occasion but without giving way to extremes of grief. At measure 9 the violin enters with a three-note motif, G–F–E♭—those notes outlining the "Lebewohl" (Farewell) motto, reminiscent of the vanishing sounds of a posthorn, that Beethoven sometimes encoded into his music, for example in the coda of the finale of the C-major Piano Concerto, Opus 15, and that he identified so conspicuously in the opening measures of the "Lebewohl" Sonata in E♭ major, Opus 81a, as a pastoral-style signifier of leave-taking.[9] Only in retrospect do we realize that the motto had already been almost invisibly pre-echoed by the piano at measure 8, in the closing phrase of the hymn, which thus is simultaneously premature disclosure and prophecy (see example 6.3).

Played *sotto voce* by the violin, the motto lasts but three measures, followed by an asymmetrical, lamenting, downward-pressing theme in the violin, a theme whose rapid figurations and exquisite chromaticisms offer a full measure of grief-laden affects before they run their course. Thus the "Lebewohl" motto emerges from the hymn and then expands into a discourse on lamentation, culminating in an ascending solo cadenza of sixty-fourth-note figures that at last delivers its fervent query to the heavens.[10] It is only following the cadenza (mm. 32–37) that the violin is finally ready to lend its voice to the hymn (mm. 38–45; see example 6.4). In a gesture of compliance, the cadenza's closing crescendo subsides into *mezza voce, semplice,* the violin thus completing the transition from bleak questioning to acceptance of the opening hymn, which it now makes its own.

To close the movement, the violin and piano in turn pursue a pastoral figure that curls gently downward from plateau to plateau (a counterbalancing response to the earlier cadenza's ascent?), perhaps seeking, without clamor, to reenter Arcadia; but having found what seems a resting place in a closing E♭ chord, played tremolo and *pianissimo* by the piano, the violin softly adds a prefiguring C♯ as though to indicate that we are not yet done, that E♭ cannot serve as a satisfactory substitute for G major, that there is more to come, that the future, importunate, is demanding its prerogatives (example 6.5).[11]

The attacca joining the Adagio espressivo to the Scherzo offers a quick passage from interiority to outwardness. Acquiescence in the congregational conception of restrained grief authorized the Scherzo's almost magical shift from despondency to celebration, made possible an emergence from the elegiac mood of the Adagio espressivo. But though the audacious C♯ lifted that mood with sleight-of-hand swiftness, the Scherzo does not by itself reestablish Arcadian harmony; rather, it constitutes an exhilarating moment en route to that restoration. Perhaps, by its nature and by its placement in classical-style structures, a scherzo must have a transitional character, or perhaps the Opus 96 sonata's narrative course cannot reach emergence all at once but must traverse several stages before eventually finding an outlet. Still, the restoration of the natural world and its simple delights is now within view, perhaps not yet here, but surely closer at hand, its nearness symbolized by an image of transparent earthly pleasure in the Trio at the Scherzo's very center—a flowing waltz in E♭ major over a bagpipe drone bass, a superlative example of one of Poggioli's "pastoral oases" (example 6.6). On the other hand, the Trio, like the scherzo of the Ninth Symphony, may be a sign not for Arcadia regained but for Arcadia's transience—a brief encounter and a quick disappearance.

EXAMPLE 6.3. Opus 96, second movement, mm. 1–13

EXAMPLE 6.4. Opus 96, second movement, mm. 33–41

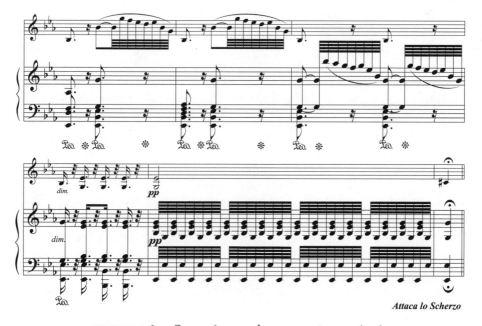

Attaca lo Scherzo

EXAMPLE 6.5. Opus 96, second movement, mm. 62–67

EXAMPLE 6.6. Opus 96, third movement, mm. 33–42

Beethoven's most inimitable scherzos are disruptive, asymmetrical, propulsively unstable, undecorous, satiric, even demonic: as one anonymous critic, writing during Beethoven's lifetime in a Vienna music journal edited by his friends and unfailingly sympathetic to his efforts, noted of this Scherzo: "It has a kind of Satyric character, with a goat's spring . . . and a rich dose of malice."[12] The critic does not say whether the maliciousness resides in the G-minor tonality or in the *sforzando-piano* syncopating strokes strategically placed on the third beat of many of its measures. In any event, the coda of this very brief Scherzo puts aside all malicious thoughts with a shift to G major that eases us into the fourth movement, Poco allegretto.

The Poco allegretto presents itself as an unproblematic set of variations on a playful, ambling theme in 2/4, a folklike dance tune alternating between the piano's treble register and the violin against a legato eighth-note pattern in the bass (example 6.7). It seems to be Beethoven's aestheticized version of a blustery buffo aria from a durable Viennese singspiel,[13] but it avoids any hint of burlesque rusticity, the swaying theme instead setting a tone of sublimated amorousness, dolce and *piano,* except for a gentle crescendo at measures 5–7 of each of its four eight-measure periods that gracefully subsides at the close of each symmetrical phrase.

Only after the theme's double bar do we realize that the music has glided into the first in a set of variations rather than a contrasting section of a finale rondo— a deceptive first impression reinforced by continuities of tempo and key as well as by the absence of a pause, let alone a full stop. Indeed, it seems that we have been lulled into thinking that there are no further serious obstacles to a felicitous out-

EXAMPLE 6.7. Opus 96, fourth movement, mm. 1–8

come: we are apparently on an unobstructed path to a place of simple, unalloyed delight. Each of the first four variations offers a different mutation of the theme's dance character. Variation 1 features a gracefully advancing and receding pattern. Variation 2, played *sempre forte,* splits the dance figures into a stamping march rhythm in the bass and a quick-time contredanse in the treble. Variation 3 accelerates the tempo with a slithering bass melody in sixteenths against light syncopations in the upper voices. And variation 4 offers eight four-measure sequences, each alternating two measures of *forte* stamping with two measures of coquettish retreat, dolce (see example 6.8), in which, to use Wilhelm von Lenz's phrase, "the dancers seek and flee one another."[14]

Despite the conventional rhetoric of these variations, however, we ought not too readily take for granted their unproblematic nature: they are not quite as straightforward or lightweight as may appear on first hearing. The unexpected intertwinings of the theme with the first variation and of each of the first three variations with its next neighbor lend a sense of continual metamorphosis to the proceedings, like a smoothly flowing relay race. The surface symmetry of the layouts is thrown into question by these intertwinings, for the closing measure of each section functions not only as an upbeat for the next but possibly as its opening as well, most strikingly where the overlapping measure seems to be integral to the rhetoric and structure of the incoming variation (see example 6.9). The double function renders the precise starting point of the new variation somewhat ambiguous. It is a musical equivalent of an optical illusion or a Moebius strip.

EXAMPLE 6.8. Opus 96, fourth movement, mm. 113–16

EXAMPLE 6.9. Opus 96, fourth movement, mm. 44–51

Moreover, the theme and its first variations are dancelike but are not identifiable dances; rather, they seem to exemplify what Kerman called "spiritualized dance parodies" that Beethoven frequently constructed to create a sense of disembodiment.[15] These tiny anomalies in structure and perception not only complicate the action but prepare for an unmistakable and dramatic (even if half-expected) event by which the finale's orbit will be thoroughly knocked off course and the structure of the sonata radically reconfigured. That moment arrives in the closing measure of variation 4, a passage in parallel motion flowing ritardando across a double bar into a section marked Adagio espressivo, thus breaking the mood, cutting the string of continuous action, and collapsing the temporal arc of the movement by a reversion to a superseded stage of the sonata's narrative trajectory—the identically titled slow movement. It is an allusion to an earlier, elegiac state of being rather than an actual repetition, creating an ambiguity that conveys a sense of enigma. Consider, for example, the extent to which the sextuplet turning figures in thirty-second notes at the end of this variation (mm. 149–63) share a density, shape, and crowded chromaticism with the sixty-fourth-note figures that close the sonata's second movement (mm. 58–64). We find ourselves within a quasi reminiscence, recalling an earlier event, but not precisely. Through this sudden reversion to inwardness, the "present" is penetrated by memories we had thought to be safely in the past.

The Adagio espressivo was deceptively half-expected, opening as though it were a conventional slow variation, intended perhaps to preface a learned-style fugal ending, to set up a gratifying close, or to prepare for the return of the tempo primo. But the highly chromaticized piano cadenzas at measures 148 and 156—bracketed by fermatas and marked crescendo-diminuendo and *langsam*[16]—derail these expectations and instead shift the scene to hypnagogic territory, drifting into an unfamiliar, dreamlike universe (example 6.10). The possibility that this is just another variation in a linear succession vanishes. Instead, Beethoven gives us something more akin to an adagio movement, thus throwing into question the form of the finale. We have been lured into deep waters.

Lenz called attention to an aberrant feature of the cadenzas, observing that each cadenza consists of three sequences of seven thirty-second notes followed by a nineteen-note passage.[17] (Alternatively, they can be counted as four sequences of seven thirty-seconds, the fourth eventuating in a twelve-note sequence.) Pressing downward from c^3 in tightly packed chromatic steps, crescendo, they are obstructed in their first three tries, but the fourth attempt succeeds, descending di-

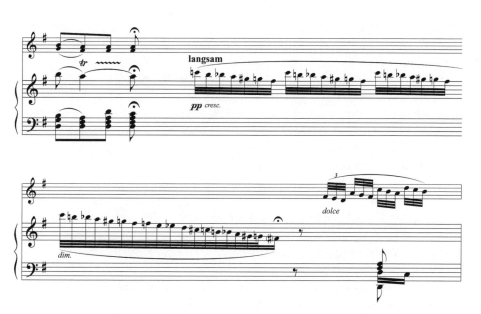

EXAMPLE 6.10. Opus 96, fourth movement, mm. 148

minuendo the rest of the way from the high f♮² to f♮¹ in an even twelve-note chromatic glide, which, after the fermata, elicits a dolce triplet passage from the violin—like a soaring bird ascending to the open sky.

After a squarely symmetrical theme and four variations, each of which lasts thirty-two measures, variation 5 occupies nineteen measures, an irregular and even enigmatic arrangement, but one appropriate to a rhapsody interlude that is heedless of exigencies of symmetry. Self-contained, a lengthy parenthesis, the Adagio espressivo variation has interrupted a story in progress, slipped into a paranormal state or hidden universe; now it is itself interrupted by two cadenzas—parentheses within a parenthesis—that calibrate the depth of a hazardous descent into remote regions. Each cadenza's densely packed chromaticisms and spiderlike falling sequences speak to dislocation, asymmetry, the traversal of uncertain terrain: they suggest the presence of an obstacle to further descent or the possibility of being trapped within a loop of repeating seven-note sequences. We have arrived at a threshold that is also a barrier to be surmounted. Having fallen into an unfamiliar universe, we now need to figure a way out.

An ending is often an ultimate object of longing, for it carries the possibility of restoration and healing. But desire cannot decide whether it prefers a happy ending or a prolongation of the now, even if the latter carries a freight of suffering. One of Beethoven's late-style answers to this conundrum is to prolong the moment, thereby delaying the ending. In any event, for Beethoven, endings ought not be too easily achieved, certainly not reachable by automatic default but only by determination, patience, and suffering, the merit badges of his Plutarchian heroism. That is a serious topic of Beethoven's late music: the construction of barriers as a necessary precondition to locating a portal, spinning a thread that leads out of a labyrinth, offering a way of returning home, healed and forgiven. A worthwhile ending therefore deserves to be postponed, kept in abeyance until the right moment.

The burden of Beethoven's Opus 96 may be that the pastoral world is neither as harmonious nor as uncomplicated as had been imagined in Haydn's oratorios or in Beethoven's own *Pastoral* Symphony. Moreover, there is no easy way to lift humanity out of the dejected state of alienation into which it has descended. Arcadia and Eden cannot be recovered without a series of trials; they are accessible only to those who have gained wisdom through hard experience, who carry memories of expulsion and exile as proofs of worthiness. Nothing but a circuitous route is adequate to so momentous an undertaking, one not unlike that of ritual initiation, which involves risks, obstacles, an awareness of deadly surprises, and even a foreboding that in the end all may be lost. The quest for an appropriate and well-earned ending requires that, as the Boyg in *Peer Gynt* understands, "You must go round about." Or as Frank Kermode once wrote, "The interest of having our expectations falsified is obviously related to our wish to reach the discovery or recognition by an unexpected and instructive route."[18]

Indeed, it requires more than a single interruption of this sonata's implied narrative to express the circuitousness of the Poco allegretto's route to realization, the density of the barrier, the twists and turns and blind alleys of the labyrinth. A crescendo-ritardando measure releases the music from the liminal sphere of the Adagio espressivo variation and at measure 164 returns it to the tempo primo, but in E♭ major, which we have by now come to understand is always transitory, whether as elegy, as Arcadian mirage, or perhaps in this instance as a marker to reassure us that the goal remains on the horizon of possibility even if the move remains premature, the ending still insufficiently prepared (see example 6.11). In its seventh measure the theme is abruptly suspended in midair, and three additional measures of rhythmic gesture prepare to catapult us back into the variation sequence, variation 6 being a whirling, madcap, allegro dance with *sforzandos* to mark the opening beats.

At measure 205 the accent shifts to the second beat, the syncopations hurtling the action forward, and then comes a learned-style fugato variation in G minor—

EXAMPLE 6.11. Opus 96, fourth movement, mm. 164–75

whose first dozen notes are identical with the movement's main theme except for
altered time values and the use of the minor mode[19]—to emphasize the gravity of
the occasion, to imply that wisdom is a precondition for a deserved pastoral ending, and in further preparation for the now considerably postponed return to the
main theme at measures 245–60.

With the return of the tempo primo in its original key, any reasonable listener
would be confident that the music is ready to end. But after sixteen bars of literal
recall of the main theme, without repeats, the music digresses into seven rushing
measures of ascending and descending scales in contrary and parallel motion,
preparing for one last postponement, a Poco adagio (mm. 275–87) that offers a
triple reminiscence—of the Adagio espressivo in this movement, which in turn is
a reminder of the elegiac second movement, and primarily of the Poco allegretto's
main theme, whose hitherto-concealed *tristesse* is now disclosed (example 6.12).

EXAMPLE 6.12. Opus 96, fourth movement, mm. 275–95

The Poco Adagio doesn't so much picture the ongoing uncertainty of the course but rather the necessity of melancholia, the impermanence of life's pleasures, the contingency of life itself. Having delivered its cautionary message, the music playfully scampers off into the sunset at measures 288–95.

Notes

1. Bion, "The Lament for Adonis," in *Theocritus, Bion, and Moschus Rendered into English Prose,* ed. and trans. Andrew Lang (London: Macmillan, 1901), 172–73.

2. See Wye Jamison Allanbrook, *Rhythmic Gesture in Mozart: "Le nozze di Figaro" and "Don Giovanni"* (Chicago: University of Chicago Press, 1983).

3. Renato Poggioli, *The Oaten Flute: Essays on Pastoral Poetry and the Pastoral Ideal* (Cambridge, Mass.: Harvard University Press, 1975), 9; see also 135–36 and 322. See also R. Curtius, *European Literature and the Latin Middle Ages,* trans. Willard R. Trask (Princeton, N.J.: Princeton University Press, 1953), chap. 10. For an eloquent discussion and brief taxonomy of such interludes, which he terms "pastoral insets," see Andrew V. Ettin, *Literature and the Pastoral* (New Haven, Conn.: Yale University Press, 1984), 75–81.

4. Allanbrook, *Rhythmic Gesture,* 131, 136, 173.

5. William Empson perceives "a natural connection between heroic and pastoral. . . . they belong to the same play—they are the two stock halves of the double plot. It is felt that you cannot have a proper hero without a proper people" (*Some Versions of Pastoral* [London, 1935; repr., Norfolk, Conn.: New Directions, 1960], 186).

6. See Leonard Ratner, *Classic Music: Expression, Form, and Style* (New York: Schirmer Books, 1980); Allanbrook, *Rhythmic Gesture;* V. Kofi Agawu, *Playing with Signs: A Semiotic Interpretation of Classic Music* (Princeton, N.J.: Princeton University Press, 1991); Adolf Sandberger, *Ausgewählte Aufsätze zur Musikgeschichte,* 2 vols. (Munich: Drei Masken, 1921, 1924), 2:201–12; Willi Kahl, "Zu Beethovens Naturauffassung," in *Beethoven und die Gegenwart: Festschrift . . . Ludwig Schiedermair,* ed. Arnold Schmitz (Berlin: Dümmlers Verlag, 1937), 220–65; F. E. Kirby, "Beethoven's Pastoral Symphony as a *Sinfonia caracteristica,*" *Musical Quarterly* 56 (1970): 605–23; Geoffrey Chew, s.v. *Pastorale,* in *The New Grove Dictionary of Music and Musicians,* ed. Stanley Sadie (London: Macmillan, 1980); idem, "The Christmas Pastorella in Austria, Bohemia, and Moravia" (Ph.D. diss., University of Manchester, 1968).

7. Gustav Nottebohm, *Zweite Beethoveniana: Nachgelassene Aufsätze* (Leipzig: C. F. Peters, 1887), 504 (my translation), 378 (trans. George Grove, *Beethoven and His Nine Symphonies,* 3d ed. [London: Novello, Ewer, 1898], 188). See also Alexander Wheelock Thayer, *Ludwig van Beethovens Leben,* rev. Hermann Deiters, ed. Hugo Riemann, 5 vols. (Leipzig: Breitkopf und Härtel, 1907–17), 3:97–98; and idem, *Thayer's Life of Beethoven,* ed. Elliot Forbes (Princeton, N.J.: Princeton University Press, 1964; rev. ed., 1967), 436. Compare the words of Johann Jakob Engel, who wrote that "the composer should always paint feelings rather than objects of feeling" (Engel, *Über die musikalische Malerey [Berlin, 1780],* qtd. and trans. in Wye J. Allanbrook, "'Ear-Tickling Nonsense': A New Context for Musical Expression in Mozart's 'Haydn' Quartets," *St. John's Review* 38 [1988]: 10). The influential theorist Johann Georg Sulzer wrote dismissively of naturalistic and imitative effects in music: "Even the most learned and skilled composers can be found doing this. But such [tone] painting violates the true spirit of music, which is to express the sentiments of feeling, not to convey images of inanimate objects" (qtd. in Nancy Kovaleff Baker and Thomas Christensen, eds., *Aesthetics and the Art of Musical Composition in the German Enlightenment: Selected Writings of Johann Georg Sulzer and Heinrich Christoph Koch* [Cambridge: Cambridge University Press, 1995], 90).

8. Early critics, such as Wilhelm von Lenz and a reviewer writing in 1819 for the *Wiener Allgemeine Musikalische Zeitung,* readily spotted the sonata's pastoral style, as did such later

writers as Herwegh, D'Indy, and Cobbett. See Wilhelm von Lenz, *Beethoven: Eine Kunst-Studie: Kritischer Katalog sämmtlicher Werke Ludwig van Beethovens mit Analysen derselben* (Hamburg: Hoffmann und Campe, 1860), vol. 4, pt. 3, pp. 267–82; anonymous reviewer for *Wiener Allgemeine Musikalische Zeitung,* in *Ludwig van Beethoven: Die Werke im Spiegel seiner Zeit: Gesammelte Konzertberichte und Rezensionen bis 1830,* ed. Stefan Kunze (Laaber: Laaber-Verlag, 1987), 324–25; Marcel Herwegh, *Technique d'interprétation sous forme d'essai d'analyse psychologique expérimental appliquée aux sonates pour piano et violon de Beethoven* (Paris: Magasin Musical, 1926), 170–78; Vincent D'Indy, *Beethoven: A Critical Biography,* trans. Theodore Baker (Boston: Boston Music, 1912), 62; Walter Willson Cobbett, comp. and ed., *Cobbett's Cyclopedic Survey of Chamber Music,* 2d ed., rev. C. Mason, 3 vols. (London: Oxford University Press, 1963), 1:91–92.

9. "Beethoven's choice of keys in his orchestral works derived from the tonal sphere of the dominant instruments" (Paul Bekker, *The Orchestra* [New York: Norton, 1936], 112). E♭ major, as a uniquely effective key for orchestrations featuring horns, becomes by association the key in which to evoke the sound of the horn, even when the music is written for other instruments.

10. In an alternative interpretation of mm. 11–14, Joseph Kerman observes that the violin's move to G–E♭–B♭ and then to B♭–A♭–G "seems to expand the horncall," transforming what could be seen as a half-expected cadential echo into a veritable "new beginning" (personal communication).

11. Denis Matthews, *Beethoven* (New York: Vintage Books, 1988), 120.

12. Anonymous reviewer for *Wiener Allgemeine Musikalische Zeitung,* qtd. in Kunze, *Beethoven,* 325.

13. Nottebohm was the first to observe similarities to "Der Knieriem bleibet, meiner Treu!" composed by J. C. Standfuss for the singspiel *Der lustige Schuster,* a sequel to *Die verwandelten Weiber oder Der Teufel ist los* (1766), which was well known through later versions of *Der lustige Schuster* with music by Johann Adam Hiller. See Gustav Nottebohm, *Beethoveniana: Aufsätze und Mittheilungen* (Leipzig: Peters, 1872), 30; see also Mary Rowen Obelkevich, "The Growth of a Musical Idea—Beethoven's Opus 96," *Current Musicology* 11 (1971): 92–93. The singspiel source is itself reminiscent of a folk tune, "Ich bin nun wie ich bin."

14. Lenz, *Kritischer Katalog,* vol. 4, pt. 3, p. 273.

15. Joseph Kerman, *The Beethoven Quartets* (New York: Knopf, 1967), 201.

16. *"Langsam"* (slowly) is apparently one of Beethoven's crucial afterthoughts, appearing in the published score but not in the original autograph.

17. Lenz, *Kritischer Katalog,* vol. 4, part 3, p. 272. He described the cadenzas as projecting "a plain tonal rapture" unique in Beethoven's music.

18. Frank Kermode, *The Sense of an Ending: Studies in the Theory of Fiction* (London: Oxford University Press, 1967), 18.

19. "The fugato subject, apparently unrelated to the rest of the movement, is none other than the first twelve notes of the variation theme played in the minor and in even eighth notes" (Warren Kirkendale, *Fugue and Fugato in Rococo and Classical Chamber Music,* trans. Margaret Bent and the author [Durham, N.C.: Duke University Press, 1979], 242–43); Lenz observed the identity of the first seven notes in *Kritischer Katalog,* vol. 4, pt. 3, p. 274n.

7. AS IF STROKED WITH A BOW: BEETHOVEN'S KEYBOARD LEGATO AND THE SONATAS FOR VIOLIN AND PIANO

Mark Kroll

The repertoire for violin and keyboard provides rich opportunities for expressive collaboration and musical dialogue. This is particularly true in works such as Beethoven's sonatas for violin and piano, in which the two instruments are given musical material of equal importance. The keyboard player, however, may experience an unaccustomed sense of intimidation when playing with a violinist, since it is a challenge to match the violin's rich palette of colors and dynamics on the piano, and especially the violinist's ability to produce a seamless legato and soaring melodic lines. This is not to discount the strengths of keyboard instruments; they are mechanical marvels capable of massive sonorities, complex contrapuntal textures, and a large range. Nevertheless, the percussive attack and rapid decay of individual tones intrinsic to the piano and, to a greater degree, the harpsichord obligates the keyboard player to exploit the full resources at his or her disposal to establish an equal musical partnership with the violin.

In a certain sense the piano was invented to address precisely this expressive incompatibility. Bartolomeo Cristofori, who is justly credited with the invention of the instrument, was fortunate to have attracted the attention of Scipione Maffei, a well-known and sometimes notorious Italian writer who assumed the role as Cristofori's unofficial publicist and public relations agent. Maffei's 1711 article "Nuova invenzione d'un gravicembalo col piano e forte" (new invention of a harpsichord with soft and loud [dynamics]) tells us that Cristofori made his piano to match the expressive powers of the violin and other string instruments heard at the "grand concertos in Rome."[1]

Since that time composers and commentators have consistently admonished the pianist to emulate the violin (as well as wind instruments and singers), particularly by playing legato. For example, George Simon Löhlein, referring to the bow stroke and slurred notes in violin performance, writes that on the keyboard "one can imitate several kinds of bowing."[2] Schindler recounts that "in *cantilena* sections" Beethoven advised people to listen "to a good violinist or wind player play it."[3] Beethoven himself added an inscription to the piano part of his song "Klage," WoO 113: "Throughout, the notes must be smooth, sustained as much as possible, and slurred together."[4] Even more pointedly, we find this inscription by Beethoven in an undated sketch for a piano work: "The difficulty here is to slur this entire passage so that the putting down of the [individual] fingers cannot be heard at all; rather, it must sound as if it were stroked with a bow."[5]

As a pianist Beethoven was renowned for his ability to achieve this effect. His legato playing was enthusiastically praised and admired by his colleagues, friends, and students, and it is acknowledged in almost every study on the composer. Nevertheless, the question still remains as to how Beethoven actually created this legato. Most commentators focus on his use of the pedals, but considerably less attention has been given to an important feature of Beethoven's approach to the piano, one that was used by almost every keyboard player in the eighteenth and early nineteenth centuries: the practice of holding down notes longer than their notated values. This technique has been called "overlegato," "superlegato," or "legatissimo." It was used not only to achieve a wide range of legato textures but also to underscore melodic and harmonic elements of a composition without resorting to the pedal or other mechanical devices. It was known and applied by harpsichordists prior to the ascendancy of the piano, and contemporary accounts of Beethoven's playing and the composer's own words confirm that it was an essential part of his pianism.

Overlegato is achieved by the fingers alone. This is consistent with the finger technique advocated by pianists through the second decade of the nineteenth century, in which the hand is kept quiet and the fingers remain close to the keys. This facet of Beethoven's performance practice has been generally overlooked, perhaps because of the almost mythic aura that surrounds the composer and the approach of modern pianists. The stereotype of the temperamental virtuoso, with his hair in disarray and his hands and arms flying about in extravagant gestures, is difficult to reconcile with the image of Beethoven sitting quietly at the piano using only his fingers. Nevertheless, there is convincing evidence that this is indeed how he played the instrument. For example, Beethoven advised players to "place the hands over the keyboard in such a way that the fingers cannot be raised more than necessary."[6] He also complained vigorously against "finger-dancing" and "manual air-sawing."[7] According to Czerny, Beethoven's "bearing was masterfully quiet, noble and beautiful, without the slightest grimace. . . . In teaching he laid great stress on a correct position of the fingers (after the school of Emanuel Bach, which he used in teaching me)."[8] In 1826 Gerhard von Breuning reported that Beethoven "held his fingers very curved . . . [in] what is called the old [hand] position."[9] Therese Brunsvik described her lessons with Beethoven in 1799, noting, "[He] never grew weary of holding down and bending my fingers, which I had been taught to lift high and hold straight."[10] Compelling testimony is added by his portrait painter Willibrord Joseph Mähler. Using the well-honed powers of observation of the visual artist, Mähler reported to Thayer that "Beethoven played with his hands so very still. . . . there was no tossing of them to and fro, up and down; they seemed to glide right and left over the keys, the fingers alone doing the work."[11]

It should come as no surprise that Beethoven played in this manner, one that is often associated with earlier music. In fact, admonitions to keep the hands and body quiet are found in every major treatise and instruction manual of the period, and this remained the standard approach to the keyboard until the time of Liszt. For example, Johann Nepomuk Hummel, a renowned pianist, an influential teacher, and a frequent colleague and competitor of Beethoven, writes that "in general, to attain the necessary facility, steadiness, and certainty . . . we must avoid every violent movement of the elbows and hands; and the muscles must not be exerted, beyond what a free and *quiet* position of the hand requires."[12] Louis Adam, the first professor of piano at the Paris Conservatoire, writes in his *Méthode:* "The hand should never disturb itself on the keyboard"; "the fingers [should be] kept very close to the keys"; "do not raise or lower the wrists too much"; "avoid all in-effective movements of the head and body"; and "all movement of the arms which is not absolutely necessary is contrary to a proper execution."[13] Pierre-Joseph-Guillman Zimmerman, Adam's successor at the Conservatoire, agreed completely.[14] He was also an advocate of the *guide-mains,* a clumsy device Friedrich Kalkbrenner invented to ensure proper hand position (Henri Herz introduced a similar contraption, which he called the "dactylion"). Even Chopin seems to have played in this manner. The drawings of Chopin at the piano by Jakob Götzenberger and Elisa Radziwill show him to be using the "older" hand and body position. It is also noteworthy that, according to Friedrich Wieck, Chopin was a great admirer of Hummel and Johann Baptist Cramer (whose legato playing, as I will show, was highly praised by Beethoven).[15]

In addition to acknowledging eyewitness reports and the force of this tradition, any consideration of Beethoven's position at the keyboard must take into account that his most important and influential teacher was Christian Gottlob Neefe. A devoted follower of C. P. E. Bach, Neefe was an organist, harpsichordist, and clavichordist, and Beethoven received his basic keyboard training in the "Leipzig" style on these very instruments. In fact, Beethoven's first duties at the Bonn court were as an organist and harpsichordist, and he was taught from the treatises of Kirnberger and Emanuel Bach, as well as the *Well-Tempered Clavier.* Furthermore, Beethoven learned piano on the Viennese instrument, which he would use primarily throughout his career. The sensitive and delicate actions of these instruments demand a subtle and refined touch, very similar to that used for the harpsichord and achieved primarily with a finger technique. It is on the Viennese piano that the application of overlegato is most useful and effective.[16]

Overlegato was a universally accepted practice for both harpsichord and piano, and descriptions of it can be found in most keyboard treatises, contemporary accounts of keyboard performance, and the prefatory material of published music.[17] In the seventeenth and eighteenth centuries it is mentioned by Nivers, Raison, Rameau, Saint-Lambert, Dornel, Türk, Milchmeyer, Knecht, and many others.[18] For example, Saint-Lambert's *Principes,* written at the apex of the grand harpsichord tradition in France, is one of the most important sources on performance practice from this period. Its explanation of overlegato is lucid and unequivocal: "All the notes that the slur encloses are played, and . . . all the notes are held after having been played, even if their value has expired, and they are only released when it is time to release the last note" (see example 7.1).[19]

Some fifty years later C. P. E. Bach, the "father" of Haydn, Mozart, and Beethoven, is equally clear in his support of overlegato. His *Versuch,* perhaps one of the most influential treatises in the history of music, was written with players of harpsichord, clavichord, and piano in mind. He describes overlegato with the following comment: "The slurred tones of broken chords are held in the manner of [example 7.2]."[20]

In the nineteenth century Adam, Hummel, and many other important contemporaries of Beethoven advocated this approach. Adam writes: "When the highest notes form a melody in those places where there is a slur, . . . all the notes may then be held under the fingers."[21] Significantly, Adam also extends the principle to diatonic motion, advising players to "keep the finger a bit on the first [note] and raise it after ½ the duration of the second" (see example 7.3).[22]

Czerny advocates overlegato for both conjunct and disjunct motion. In one example he writes, "The notes of the melody [i.e., diatonic] in the right hand must be held down so long, that each finger shall not quit its key till somewhat after the next note is struck."[23]

EXAMPLE 7.1 Saint-Lambert, *Principes du clavecin,* p. 29

EXAMPLE 7.2 C. P. E. Bach, *Versuch über die wahre Art,* p. 155

EXAMPLE 7.3 Louis Adam, *Méthode,* article sept, p. 151

Hummel adds authoritative support to the use of overlegato in his monumental treatise. He confirms that "the hand must never leave the keyboard. The liaisons are only done with the fingers glued to the keys."[24] He later describes one of the basic principles of overlegato: "There are certain groups of notes which include a melody, and which must not be played detached. . . . the delivery of them must be connected, and the melody brought out" (see example 7.4).[25] It is worth pointing out that Hummel, like many composer-pianists of the time, was also an accomplished violinist.

In addition to the substantial documentation, practical and empirical evidence must also be considered. That is, performers who have applied this technique when playing the harpsichord, clavichord, organ, and fortepiano will recognize that overlegato is an effective, natural, and idiomatic technique for playing expressively. Drawing on a thirty-year career as a performing harpsichordist and fortepianist, I can attest to the efficacy and wide applicability of overlegato. It has been essential in my ability to achieve subtle legato nuances and inflections on the keyboard, whether playing a François Couperin *pièce de clavecin,* the harpsichord part to the sonatas for violin and harpsichord of J. S. Bach, or Beethoven's violin and piano sonatas. It is independent of the use of harpsichord registrations or piano pedaling.

In terms of the piano, the legato and overlegato created by the fingers alone is quite different from that achieved by the use of the damper pedal. This is an important distinction, particularly relevant to modern pianists, who are accustomed to playing legato primarily with the pedal. Certainly the damper pedal was an im-

EXAMPLE 7.4 Hummel, *A Complete Theoretical . . . ,* pt. 3, sec. 2, ch. 2, p. 60

portant device and a valid part of the pianist's technique, even in the early days of the instrument. Nonetheless, the debate over its use and abuse was considerable. Most teachers and writers from the period caution against relying on it, especially to achieve a *forte* dynamic, and they criticize players who use it to cover up deficiencies in their technique and musicianship. Hummel, for example, writes: "A truly great Artist has no occasion for Pedals to work upon his audience by expression and power. . . . Neither Mozart, nor Clementi, required these helps to obtain the highly deserved reputation of [being] the greatest and most expressive performers of their day."[26] Gardeton writes: "It is rare that the great pianists make use of their help; they generally regard this mechanism as more suitable for producing confusion in the harmony; for introducing variety into the performance. . . . Clever masters wish, so to speak, that *the pedals are only to be found at the end of their fingertips.*"[27] Dussek believed that excessive use of the pedal is "a sure proof of the want of a good finger."[28] On the whole the Viennese school of piano playing was quite conservative with regard to the use of the pedal. Even in 1830 Kalkbrenner was reporting that "in Germany the use of the pedals is scarcely known."[29] This was admittedly something of an overstatement at that late date. There were certainly advocates on both sides. The leading proponents of pedaling, Milchmeyer and Daniel Steibelt (*Méthode du piano* [Paris and Leipzig, 1809]), were both excellent musicians and writers but nevertheless seem to have become obsessed with the "new toy" aspect of this mechanism. In his treatise Milchmeyer in particular writes extensively about the use of the damper pedal and the exploitation of every other possible "mutation" on the instrument. At one point he even offers unintentionally comic instructions about manually raising and lowering the piano lid to create extreme dynamic effects. Not surprisingly, such an approach inspired a strong reaction, and many observers accused those who abused the pedals of "charlatanism." A contemporary reviewer complained vigorously about Milchmeyer's pedal fixation: "This must be the worst chapter in the whole work. The author recommends the purchase of small square pianos—why? Because there are more stops and mutations on them!" He goes on to add, pointedly: "We Germans would rather stick by our Stein instruments, on which we can do everything without stops."[30]

Nevertheless, whether the pedal was used incorrectly or too often is not the issue here and misses an essential point. Since overlegato was an accepted and integral part of keyboard technique when Beethoven was active as a pianist, it is important to examine how to play in this manner *without* using the pedal. This is true for all of Beethoven's keyboard parts, and it is relevant when performing on either fortepiano or the modern instrument.

That legato playing was an integral part of Beethoven's initial conception of music is evident in the early sketches. For one example, he directs the player to "keep the hand [as quiet] and held close as is possible," and to maintain "the strictest legato."[31] In another sketch he offers an uncommon but specific fingering that has inspired a number of conflicting interpretations. Beethoven writes: "Here the 3d finger must lie across the 4th as long [as possible], until it moves away and the 3d can take its place" (example 7.5).[32]

EXAMPLE 7.5 Beethoven, early sketch

Some commentators believe that the composer here is asking for a finger substitution, an exchange of fingers on the same key before moving to the next note. Players of early pianos and the harpsichord, however, will recognize an alternative interpretation. With the shallow key dips and light actions of these instruments, this fingering enables the player to repeat the same note with an approximation of legato by "catching" the damper before it can fully dampen the vibrations of the string. It is further evidence of Beethoven's desire to achieve the utmost in legato, even between two repeated notes, and of his command of the piano as it existed in his lifetime.

This fingering has ample historical precedent and recalls a section in François Couperin's *L'Art de toucher le clavecin* in which he tells the student to change fingers on repeated notes, in a manner similar to that suggested by Beethoven's instruction, to achieve the best legato. Charmingly, Couperin adds that he could tell if a player was using this fingering even when he had his back turned.[33] A further confirmation of Beethoven's obsession with legato, and his roots in the harpsichord and organ, comes from Schindler, who remembered that Beethoven was once an organist. He writes: "In regard to his sustained style, . . . we see the former organist."[34]

An excellent source of information about Beethoven's application of legato and overlegato can be found in his written comments to the Cramer Etudes. Cramer's piano playing was admired by Beethoven and many other pianists of the time, including Moscheles. As Ernst Pauer wrote: "Beethoven preferred Cramer's touch to all others; the quietness, smoothness, the pliability of the movements of his hands and fingers, the exceptional clearness. . . . All who had the good fortune to hear Cramer play, speak of his legato and adagio playing with rapture."[35] Czerny noted that the finale to Beethoven's Piano Sonata, Opus 26, was inspired in part by Cramer, whose visit to Vienna in 1799–1800 prompted Beethoven to write this work.[36] Schindler writes: "In our master's opinion, these études contained all the fundamentals of good piano playing. . . . because of the polyphony used in many of them, he considered them the best preparations for the playing of his own works."[37]

Beethoven wanted the Etudes used to teach his nephew Karl, so he was particularly concerned that they be exploited to their full advantage. His inscriptions therefore provide invaluable insights into his own technique and musical thinking. The Cramer Etudes inscriptions also let us glimpse into Beethoven's analytical mind, seeing how he understood all the implications and essential elements of a musical phrase. They should be clear and logical to every pianist and ring true from both musical and practical perspectives.[38] Let us examine a few of these annotated etudes.

For a passage in Etude no. 1 Beethoven writes, "In order to obtain the necessary binding [in both the technical and musical senses of the term] the finger must not be lifted off the first note of each group until the fourth note is to be struck"[39] (see example 7.6). Here at the very outset is incontrovertible evidence that overlegato was used in diatonic motion, for structural purposes, and not only for the notes of a chord to enhance its color and sonority. A similar instance can be found in Etude no. 3. Beethoven writes, "On account of binding, the finger should dwell on this [i.e., first] accented note" of the group (see example 7.7).

In Etude no. 2 Beethoven describes one of the most common applications of overlegato: "In the four introductory bars the thumb adheres firmly to the fundamental note, so that the broken triads, and in a similar manner all broken chords may be made clear" (example 7.8). This is done "to obtain binding."

The other commonly held principle, of holding down the notes of an implied melody (cf. Hummel and Adam), can be found in Etude no. 7 (example 7.9). Beethoven writes: "The finger continues to dwell, for the space of two (eighth notes) on the long syllable (first note)."

With Etude no. 5 Beethoven seems to be working backward (example 7.10). That is, his inscription is added to confirm what he already considers common performance practice: "Were, however, [all the sixteenth notes connected in one

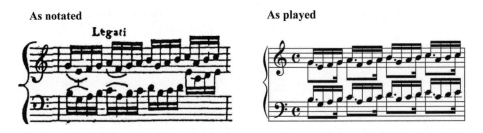

EXAMPLE 7.6 Cramer/Beethoven, Etude No. 1

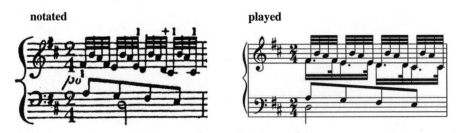

EXAMPLE 7.7 Cramer/Beethoven, Etude No. 3

notated **played**

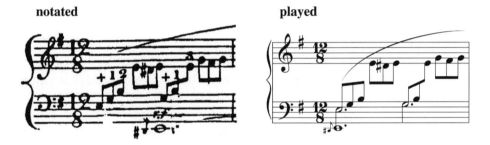

EXAMPLE 7.8 Cramer/Beethoven, Etude No. 2

notated **played**

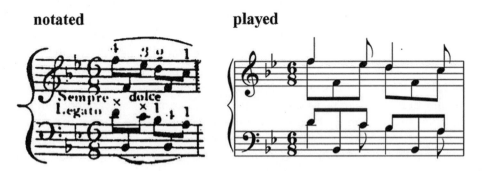

EXAMPLE 7.9 Cramer/Beethoven, Etude No. 7

Notated and Played **Simplifed Notation**

EXAMPLE 7.10 Cramer/Beethoven, Etude No. 5

brace] still the first note of each group would have to be uniformly accentuated and held down."

One of the most often cited of these etudes, number 24, is perhaps the best example of the use of structural overlegato (example 7.11). Here Beethoven writes that "the first note of the first triplet and the third note of the second triplet must be connected together . . . so that the melody may stand out."

The remainder of the annotated etudes fully support and amplify what is clear and unquestionable—Beethoven used overlegato consistently and frequently. It should be further underscored that Beethoven never speaks of using the pedal here. He refers to the fingers alone.

Did Beethoven or other composers use a system of notation that clearly indicates where overlegato should be applied? Unfortunately, notation has always been an imperfect and incomplete guide for performers. Overdotting and the use and degree of *inégal* in French baroque music are just two areas where confusion has resulted from this problem. Touch and articulation are even more resistant to unambiguous notation. Although many writers from the period explained the meanings of the three signs for a detached performance (i.e., the wedge, the dot, and the dot under a slur), even here there is no unanimous agreement. We have an almost infinite variety of staccato touches that cannot be measured; they depend on such factors as the musical context, the individual instrument, or the acoustics of the hall. The same is true regarding legato. We have only one sign for a slur, but legato playing can span the gamut from holding down all the notes with the damper pedal engaged to the slightest hint of overlegato.

It is true that Beethoven was quite specific and generous in his notation of slurs for all his music. According to William Newman, "Beethoven marked slurs in his scores more extensively and more regularly than any other great master had done before him."[40] Slurs and their accurate notation were important to Beethoven, as he forcefully expresses in a letter to Karl Holz of 15 August 1825: "For God's sake please impress on Rampl to copy everything exactly as it stands. . . . The slurs

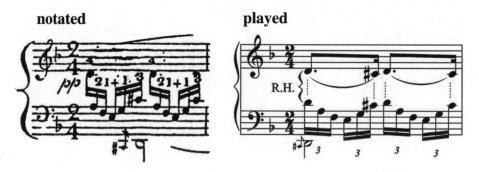

EXAMPLE 7.11 Cramer/Beethoven, Etude No. 24

should be exactly as they are now. It is not all the same whether it is like this 𝅘𝅥𝅮𝅘𝅥𝅮 or like this 𝅘𝅥𝅮𝅘𝅥𝅮."[41] Nevertheless, the sign for a slur does not provide sufficient information, and any attempt to notate overlegato would be excessively complicated and counterproductive, as witnessed by my realizations for the musical examples here. Rather, pianists can establish a reasonable and coherent basis on which to decide where they can and should use overlegato by carefully reading and interpreting Beethoven's notation, applying our knowledge of performance practice, and analyzing the harmonic, melodic, and structural implications of the music itself.

Music for keyboard with a string instrument provides an excellent context in which to examine the use of overlegato. This is particularly true of Beethoven's violin and piano sonatas, which from the earliest (Opus 12) to the last (Opus 96) contain literally hundreds of passages that benefit from the technique. Let us examine some of these passages.

In example 7.12 the use of the pedal to achieve legato in the left hand would prevent the pianist from playing the right hand unslurred, as Beethoven has notated. The use of overlegato in the left hand will not only create the variety of touch between the two hands but also underscore the implied melody in the lower part. The same is true in example 7.13, except that the right hand must be played overlegato. Finally, in example 7.14, use of overlegato will allow the right-hand notes 1 and 2 to be played staccato and notes 3 and 4 legato while the melodic and harmonic implications of the left-hand accompaniment figure are highlighted.

Example 7.15 is a classic example of the use of overlegato. Complete "binding" can be achieved in each of the hands without destroying the articulations created by the eighth-note rests. In example 7.16, moreover, the delicate opening to the third movement of Opus 12, No. 2, Beethoven precisely notates a wide range of articulations and slurring to create wonderfully subtle effects of accent and phrasing. This would be lost if the pedal were used throughout.

In example 7.17 Beethoven uses both long and short articulations in the right hand, while the regular accompaniment figure requires one of the traditional applications of overlegato. In example 7.18 the first two notes of the right hand in

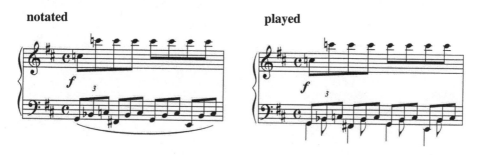

EXAMPLE 7.12 Beethoven, Opus 12, No. 1, first movement, m. 70

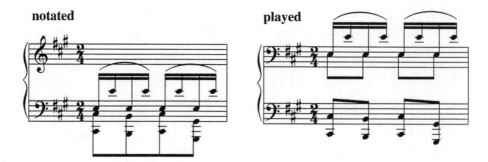

EXAMPLE 7.13 Beethoven, Opus 12, No. 1, second movement, m. 11

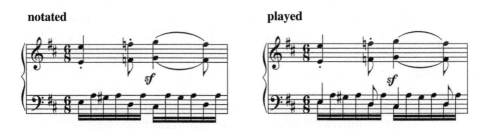

EXAMPLE 7.14 Beethoven, Opus 12, No. 1, third movement, m. 36

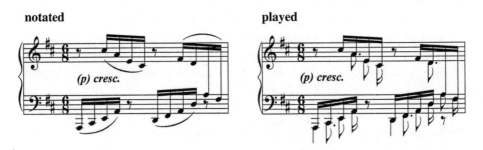

EXAMPLE 7.15 Beethoven, Opus 12, No. 1, third movement, m. 44

notated

played

EXAMPLE 7.16 Beethoven, Opus 12, No. 2, third movement, mm.1–4

measures 20 and 21 must be slurred, since they are appogiatura figures, but there must be a separation before the second half of beat 3 in each measure. At the same time, an articulation is needed between beats 1 and 2 of the left hand of measure 20, while beats 2–4 are connected. Although this can be accomplished by some complicated "syncopated" pedaling, overlegato will achieve it more clearly and easily. In the passage shown in example 7.19, the left hand demands the utmost in legato performance throughout, but there is an articulation between the first and second notes of the right hand and before beat 3. Compare this with measure 2 of the same movement (example 7.20), where the pedal can be used throughout.

In example 7.21, from the second movement of Opus 24, Beethoven could have written a slur over the sextuplet and triplet figures in the right hand, but he preferred a more articulated performance of the passage. The only way to achieve this while maintaining a complete legato in the movement's predominant left-hand accompaniment figure is to employ overlegato in that hand. In example 7.22, from the third movement, both types of conventional overlegato seem appropriate; that is, for the diatonic motion in the right hand and the chordal writing in the left. The player is also able to perform beats 3 and 4 of the right-hand staccato, as indicated, while keeping the left hand connected.

Yet another example of achieving legato in one hand and detaché in the other occurs in the third movement of Opus 24 (example 7.23), and in the fourth movement we again observe one of the standard and effective uses of overlegato (example 7.24). Employing the pedal throughout the measure would result in a loss of the articulation needed for the rhythmic accents between strong and weak beats. The application of overlegato in example 7.25 is similar to that in example

EXAMPLE 7.17 Beethoven, Opus 12, No. 2, third movement, mm. 66–71

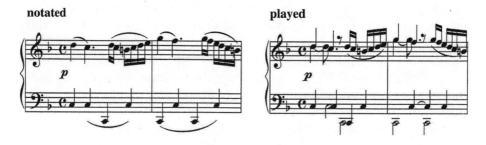

EXAMPLE 7.18 Beethoven, Opus 24, first movement, mm. 20–21

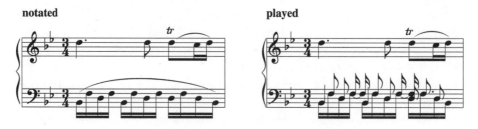

EXAMPLE 7.19 Beethoven, Opus 24, second movement, m. 4

EXAMPLE 7.20 Beethoven, Opus 24, second movement, m. 2

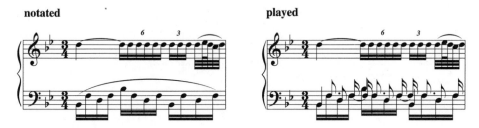

EXAMPLE 7.21 Beethoven, Opus 24, second movement, m. 30

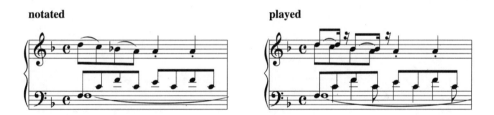

EXAMPLE 7.22 Beethoven, Opus 24, third movement, m. 1

7.18. It is noteworthy that the technique is still useful in this, the last of Beethoven's sonatas for violin and piano. The use of overlegato in example 7.26, particularly in the left hand, recalls Beethoven's instructions for Cramer's Etudes nos. 3 and 24. The apparent dissonances created by holding down these notes will be less noticeable on the early piano, with its rapid decay, and certainly less than if the pedal were to be used throughout this passage. In example 7.27, the final excerpt from Opus 96, overlegato will enable the pianist to play the right hand connected and the left hand with its clearly notated staccato.

Finally, any discussion of the practical and technical aspects of overlegato must be placed within the larger context of the history of piano technique. The development of musical styles is rarely a smooth and seamless chain of interdependent

EXAMPLE 7.23 Beethoven, Opus 24, third movement, m. 190

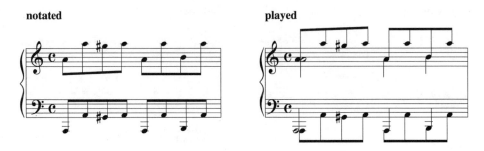

EXAMPLE 7.24 Beethoven, Opus 47, fourth movement, m. 48

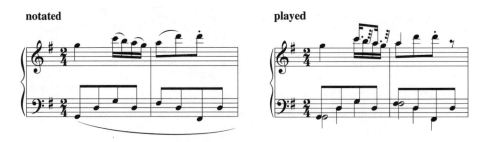

EXAMPLE 7.25 Beethoven, Opus 96, fourth movement, mm. 1–2

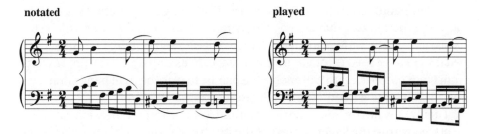

EXAMPLE 7.26 Beethoven, Opus 96, fourth movement, mm. 81–82

notated   **played**

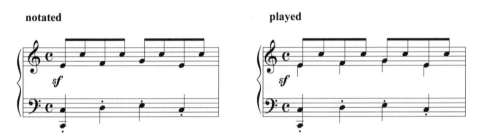

EXAMPLE 7.27 Beethoven, Opus 96, fourth movement, m. 270

events, and this is certainly true with regard to keyboard playing. The second and third decades of the nineteenth century witnessed a dramatic, quantum shift in the way the piano was played, one that directly parallels the ascendancy of the "symphonic ideal" for which that century has been recognized. For the first time the piano was considered to be not only a solo or chamber music instrument but one that could express and match the power and timbres of the orchestra. The group of young Turks who transformed the technique and the instrument included Chopin, Thalberg, and most of all Liszt. For Liszt, the entire range of the piano (and more) and all its resources (e.g., pedals, louder dynamics, and heavier stringing) were there to be exploited and stretched to or beyond their limits. Fingers, arms, feet, and any other body parts were all fair game.

Changes in piano construction reflected and influenced this transformation. After Beethoven's death the English piano, with its heavier action, deeper key dip, and tendency to favor volume over articulation, gradually supplanted the Viennese piano that Beethoven preferred. The German *"sprechend"* style of playing, with its emphasis on rhetorical gesture, also lost favor as an aesthetic ideal. Many subtleties of touch and articulation, such as overlegato, were considered by later generations to be exceptions to the rule or old-fashioned.

Contemporary musicians and commentators were well aware that a major change was happening during their lifetimes. For example, Czerny reflected on the basic styles: "Clementi's style . . . , Cramer and Dussek's style . . . , Mozart's school . . . , and the Beethoven style." There is then "the modern brilliant school founded by Hummel, Kalkbrenner and Moscheles. . . . Out of these schools, a new style is just now beginning to be developed, which may be called a mixture of and improvement on all those which preceded it. It is chiefly represented by Thalberg, Chopin, Liszt and other young artists."[42] Of Henselt, Czerny observes that his "way at the keyboard may be taken as the link between Hummel's and Liszt's; that is to say, with Hummel's strictly legato touch, quiet hands and strong fingers, Henselt produced effects of rich sonority something like those which Liszt got with the aid of the wrists and pedals." He also *"had a way of holding the keys down as much as possible with the fingers."*[43]

François-Joseph Fétis, that perceptive and sometimes prophetic musicologist of the 1840s, describes this phenomenon clearly and extensively in his *Méthode des méthodes*. He writes: "There are also peculiar contrivances in the performance of Liszt, although of another kind, and his genius is the most complete deviation . . . from the school of Hummel that one can imagine. Delicacy of touch is not the principal object of his [Liszt's] talent, and his ideas are directed toward increasing the powers of the piano and toward the necessity of making it, as much as possible, resemble the effect of an orchestra. Hence those particular combinations produced by the frequent employment of the pedals and the special ways of striking the keys."[44] Or as Frederick Niecks said succinctly: "It was not until the time of Liszt, Thalberg and Chopin that the pedals became a power in pianoforte playing."[45]

All this evidence has significant implications for our understanding and performance of Beethoven and the keyboard music of his contemporaries. Pianists (and the piano) up to and through the time of Beethoven were inextricably linked to earlier harpsichord, clavichord, and organ traditions, and the aesthetic goals for these composers and players were not orchestral but pianistic. Whether the music of this period is performed today on the modern or period instrument, pianists will find the techniques described here to be instructive and historically relevant. Moreover, since most pianists receive their basic and earliest training on the modern instrument in the post-Lisztian tradition, it should be recognized that this influence can still remain even after the most intensive and dedicated study of early pianos and historical performance practices.[46] For example, I am reminded of a statement by William Newman, in which he suggests that a passage in the finale of the Piano Sonata, Opus 28, should be played using the "dog-paddle" technique.[47] Newman here is referring to the technique on the modern piano in which the hands, arms, and shoulders are used freely, in a manner resembling that of a dog paddling in the water; the fingers play a minor role; and the pedal serves to achieve legato. In other words, he is interpreting and playing early nineteenth-century piano music with the hindsight of twentieth-century practice.[48]

The novelist James Baldwin eloquently observed that the artist "lays bare the questions which have been hidden by the answers."[49] This is certainly true for performers who, as they strive to learn and re-create musical works, must always be aware that great art asks more questions than it answers. In terms of my discussion, I am not suggesting that the piano should be played without pedal or the many other techniques in use today.[50] Nor was Beethoven insensitive to the transformation that occurred in the piano and piano playing during his lifetime. I do propose, however, that pianists would do well to acknowledge a keyboard technique indebted to centuries of tradition, rethink their dependence on the pedal and other practices of the late nineteenth century, and put full faith and trust in the devices for which the piano is so well suited—the fingers.

Notes

1. Scipione Maffei, "Nuova invenzione d'un gravicembalo col piano e forte," *Giornale de'letterati d'Italia 5* (1711): 144–59 (my translation).

2. George Simon Löhlein, *Clavier-Schule* (Leipzig: Waisenhaus und Fromman, 1765), 69; qtd. and trans. in Sandra P. Rosenblum, *Performance Practices in Classic Piano Music* (Bloomington: Indiana University Press, 1988), 174.

3. Anton F. Schindler, *Biographie von Ludwig van Beethoven*, 2d ed. (Münster: Aschendorff, 1840); English-language translation of 3d ed., Schindler, *Beethoven as I Knew Him*, trans. Constance Jolly, ed. Donald W. MacArdle (Chapel Hill: University of North Carolina Press, 1966), 416.

4. "Durchaus müssen die Töne geschliffen und so sehr als möglich ausgehalten und zusammengebunden werden" (*Beethoven Werke: Gesamtausgabe, Supplement,* ser. 25, no. 283 [Leipzig: Breitkopf und Härtel, 1949], 269; qtd. and trans. in Rosenblum, *Performance Practices,* 152). This instruction is written into the piano part, mm. 1–4.

5. "Das Schwere hierbei ist, diese ganze Passage so zu schliefen, dass man das Aufsetzen der Finger gar nicht hören kann, sondern, al wenn mit dem Bogen gestrichen würde, so muss es klingen" (Theodor von Frimmel, *Beethoven-Studien,* 2 vols. [Munich: Müller, 1905, 1906], 2:214; qtd. in Rosenblum, *Performance Practices,* 152; my translation).

6. Schindler, *Biographie,* vol. 2, p. 228; qtd. and trans. in Rosenblum, *Performance Practices,* 194 .

7. Qtd. and trans. in Rosenblum, *Performance Practices,* 194.

8. Qtd. in Alexander Thayer, *Thayer's Life of Beethoven,* ed. Elliot Forbes (Princeton, N.J.: Princeton University Press, 1964), 368–69.

9. Gerhard von Breuning, *Aus dem Schwarzspanierhause: Erinnerungen an Ludwig van Beethoven aus meiner Jugendzeit* (Vienna, 1874; facs. repr., Hildesheim: Georg Olms, 1970), 106; qtd. in Gerhard von Breuning, *Memories of Beethoven,* trans. Henry Mins and Maynard Solomon, ed. Maynard Solomon (Cambridge: Cambridge University Press, 1972), 78.

10. Qtd. in Thayer, *Life,* 235.

11. Qtd. in ibid., 337.

12. J. N. Hummel, *A Complete Theoretical and Practical Course of Instructions, on the Art of Playing the Piano Forte* (London: T. Boosey, 1827?/1828), pt. 1, sec. 1, chap. 2, pp. 3–4 (emphasis added). For a full discussion of Hummel's treatise, see Mark Kroll, "La Belle Exécution," in *Historical Musicology: Sources, Methods, Interpretations,* ed. Stephen Crist and Roberta Marvin (Rochester, N.Y.: University of Rochester Press, forthcoming).

13. Louis Adam, *Méthode de piano du Conservatoire* (Paris: Magasin de Musique du Conservatoire Royal, 1804; facs. repr., Geneva: Minkoff, 1974) (my translations): "le main ne doit jamais se déranger sur le clavier" and "les doigts très serrés sur les touches" (article sept, 151); "ne pas trop lever ni baisser le poignet," "éviter les mouvements inutile de tête et de corps," and "Tout mouvement des bras qui n'est absolutment nécessaire est préjudicable à l'éxecution" (article trois, 7).

14. Pierre-Joseph-Guillman Zimmerman, *Encyclopédie du Pianiste—Compositeur* (Paris: L'Auteur, 1840).

15. Wieck's piano method of 1853 is aptly titled *Clavier und Gesang;* see Friedrich Wieck, *Piano and Song,* ed. Nancy Reich (New York: Da Capo, 1982).

16. Distinctions between the actions of English and Viennese pianos were frequently acknowledged throughout the period, and each type found its advocates. Briefly stated, English actions tended to be heavier and with a deeper key dip than their Viennese counterparts, but they had a fuller sonority. Most pianists outside England, at least prior to the 1820s, seemed to prefer the Viennese instrument, but touring virtuosos were always careful to be

both accommodating and diplomatic. Hummel, for example, devotes an entire chapter to the subject (see Hummel, *Complete Theoretical,* pt. 3, sec. 2, chap. 4, p. 64).

17. I am disappointed that this practice is still not fully recognized. For example, I once lectured on keyboard touch and articulation at the 1985 Aston Magna Academy, where I discussed the technique of sustaining two or more notes longer than their written values. To my surprise, an organist with a supposedly good historical performance background excitedly interrupted with the question, "You mean at the same time?"

18. Guillaume Nivers, *Livre d'orgue* (1665), preface; André Raison, *Livre d'orgue* (1688), preface; J. P. Rameau, *Pièces de clavessin* (1724), introduction; Michel de Saint-Lambert, *Principes du clavecin* (1702); Charles Dornel, *Pièces de clavecin* (1731); Daniel Gottlob Türk, *Klavierschule, oder Anweisung zum Klavierspielen für Lehrer und Lernende* (1789, 1802); Johann Peter Milchmeyer: *Die wahre Art das Pianoforte zu Spielen* (1797); Justin Heinrich Knecht, *Vollständige Orgelschule* (1795).

19. Michel de Saint-Lambert, *Principles of the Harpsichord,* trans. and ed. Rebecca Harris-Warrick (Cambridge: Cambridge University Press, 1984), chap. 7, p. 29.

20. Carl Philipp Emanuel Bach, *Versuch über die wahre Art das Clavier zu spielen* (Berlin: in Verlegung des Auctoris, 1753); English-language edition, C. P. E. Bach, *Essay on the True Art of Playing Keyboard Instruments,* trans. and ed. William Mitchell (New York: Norton, 1949), 155.

21. "Quand les notes les plus hautes peuvent former un chant dans les endroits où il y a une liaison . . . , on peut tenir alors, toutes les notes sous les doigts" (Adam, *Méthode,* article sept, 151; my translation).

22. "appuyer un peu le doigt sur la première et le lever à la seconde en lui ôtant la moité de sa valeur" (ibid.; my translation).

23. Carl Czerny, *Theoretical and Practical Piano Forte School,* trans. J. A. Hamilton (London: R. Cocks, 1839), 21.

24. Hummel, *Complete Theoretical,* pt. 1, sec. 2, chap. 2, p. 24.

25. Ibid., pt. 3, sec. 2, chap. 2, p. 60.

26. Ibid., pt. 3, sec. 2, chap. 3, p. 62.

27. C. Gardeton, *Almanach de la musique pour l'an 1819* (Paris, 1820), 261; qtd. and trans. in David Rowland, *A History of Pianoforte Pedalling* (Cambridge: Cambridge University Press, 1993), 115 (emphasis added).

28. Dussek qtd. in W. Nicholson, *The British Encyclopaedia* (London, 1809), s.v. *Musical Instruments;* qtd. in Rowland, *A History,* 40.

29. Friedrich Kalkbrenner, *Méthode pour apprendre le pianoforte* (Paris: M. Schlesinger, 1830); English-language edition (Kalkbrenner, *A New Method of Studying the Piano-Forte* [London: D'Almain, 1832], 10) qtd. in Rowland, *A History,* 35.

30. *Allgemeine Musikalische Zeitung,* 21 November 1798, p. 136; qtd. and trans. in Rowland, *A History,* 40.

31. "Die Hand so sehr als möglich zusammen gehalten" and "auf das strengste ligato" (Gustav Nottebohm, *Zweite Beethoveniana: Nachgelassene Aufsätze* [Leipzig: C. F. Peters, 1887], 362 [my translation]).

32. "Hierbei muss der 3te Finger über dem 4ten so lange kreuzweis liegen, bis dieser wegzieht und alsdann der 3te an seine Stelle kömmt" (Nottenbohm, *Zweite Beethoveniana,* 363; my translation).

33. François Couperin, *L'Art de toucher le clavecin* (Paris: chés M. Couperin, 1716; rev. ed. 1717); modern ed., ed. Anna Linde (Wiesbaden: Breitkopf und Härtel, 1933, 1961), 16–17.

34. Schindler, *Beethoven as I Knew Him,* 415.

35. Ernst Pauer, *The Art of Pianoforte Playing* (London: Novello, 1877), 36.

36. Carl Czerny, "On the Proper Performance of All Beethoven's Works for Piano Solo,"

chaps. 2 and 3 of *The Art of Playing the Ancient and Modern Piano Works* (London: Cocks, 1846); facsimile repr., *On the Proper Performance of All Beethoven's Works for Piano Solo,* ed. Paul Badura-Skoda (Vienna: Universal-Edition, 1970), 38; qtd. in Rosenblum, *Performance Practices,* 101.

37. Schindler, *Beethoven as I Knew Him,* 379.

38. Many questions have been raised about the authenticity of these notations, including the supposition that Schindler might have written them himself. The exhaustive study by Dagmar Beck and Grita Herre, "Anton Schindlers 'Nutzanwendung' der Cramer-Etüden," in *Zu Beethoven,* ed. H. Goldschmidt (Berlin: Verlag Neue Musik, 1988), 177–208, presents a convincing case that many of Schindler's comments are indeed forgeries. Nevertheless, Schindler did play the piano for Beethoven, frequently listened to the composer, and was intimately familiar with the styles of piano performance throughout Beethoven's life and in subsequent generations. Therefore, even if these annotations do not represent Beethoven's actual words, it is reasonable to assume that they reflect the approach to music and the piano that Beethoven and many of his contemporaries favored. In the context of the violin and piano sonatas, it should be noted that Schindler was also a good violinist who served as concertmaster of the Josephstadt Theater orchestra.

39. This and all other translations of the annotations are from J. S. Shedlock, "Beethoven as a Piano Teacher," in *The Beethoven Companion,* ed. Thomas K. Scherman and Louis Biancolli (Garden City, N.Y.: Doubleday, 1972), 419–22.

40. William Newman, *Beethoven on Beethoven* (New York: Norton, 1988), 123.

41. Ludwig van Beethoven, *Briefwechsel Gesamtausgabe,* ed. Sieghard Brandenburg, 7 vols. (Munich: G. Henle Verlag, 1996–98), vol. 6, no. 2032; English-language translation, Beethoven, *The Letters of Beethoven,* trans. and ed. Emily Anderson, 3 vols. (London: Macmillan, 1961), no. 1421.

42. Carl Czerny, *Vollständige theoretische-practische Pianoforteschule, op. 500,* vol. 3 (Vienna: Diabelli, 1839); English-language translation, trans. J. A. Hamilton (London: Cocks, 1939), qtd. in Rowland, *A History,* 107.

43. Grove, ed., *A Dictionary of Music and Musicians,* s.v. *Henselt;* qtd. in Rowland, *A History,* 118 (emphasis added).

44. "Il y aussi des procédés dans le jeu de Liszt, mais ils sont d'autre nature, et son talent est la déviation la plus complète . . . qu'on puisse imaginer de l'école de Hummel. La délicatesse du toucher n'est pas l'object principal de son talent, et ses vues se portent sur l'augmentation de puissance du piano, et sur la nécessité de rapprocher cette puissance de celle de l'orchestre, autant qu'il est possible. De là certaines combinaisons qui lui sont particulières de l'emploi fréquent des pédales avec des procédés spéciaux d'attaque des touches" (François-Joseph Fétis and Ignaz Moscheles, *Méthode des méthodes* [Paris: M. Schlesinger, 1840; facs. repr., Geneva: Minkoff, 1973], 3 [my translation]).

45. Qtd. in Rowland, *A History,* 108.

46. This is not always the case. The legendary pianist Artur Schnabel was reported to have said that "the pedal is very seldom used in the classic piano literature as a means of coloring" (qtd. in Harold Schoenberg, "The Pianist," in *The Beethoven Reader,* ed. Dennis Arnold and Nigel Fortune [New York: Norton, 1971], 107).

47. Newman, *Beethoven,* 282.

48. The use and value of overlegato were not completely forgotten or discounted in the twentieth and twenty-first centuries. One confirmation of this comes to us from an unlikely source—the noted theorist Heinrich Schenker. In his little-known work *The Art of Performance* (trans. Irene Schreier Scott, ed. Heribert Esser [New York: Oxford University Press, 2000]), Schenker discusses the importance of overlegato in great detail, calling it the "hand pedal." Significantly, he also urges pianists to emulate the expressive potential of the vio-

lin and the human voice. I am grateful to Professors Nicholas Cook and William Drabkin for bringing this to my attention

49. James Baldwin, "Creative Process," in *Creative America* (New York: Ridge, 1962), 17–21; qtd. in Kenneth Drake, *The Sonatas of Beethoven as He Played and Taught Them* (Bloomington: Indiana University Press, 1972), 196.

50. Beethoven did insert more than eight hundred pedal indications in his music, and the pedal is one of the basic elements of any pianist's technique.

Bibliography

Adam, Louis. *Méthode de piano du Conservatoire.* Paris: Au Magasin de musique du Conservatoire royal, 1804. Reprint, Geneva: Minkoff, 1974.

Agawu, V. Kofi. *Playing with Signs: A Semiotic Interpretation of Classic Music.* Princeton, N.J.: Princeton University Press, 1991.

Ahn, Suhnne. "Genre, Style, and Compositional Procedure in Beethoven's 'Kreutzer' Sonata, Opus 47." Ph.D. diss., Harvard University, 1997.

Albrecht, Theodore, ed. *Letters to Beethoven.* Lincoln: University of Nebraska Press, 1996.

Allanbrook, Wye Jamison. "'Ear-Tickling Nonsense': A New Context for Musical Expression in Mozart's 'Haydn' Quartets." *St. John's Review* 38 (1988): 10.

———. *Rhythmic Gesture in Mozart: "Le nozze di Figaro" and "Don Giovanni."* Chicago: University of Chicago Press, 1983.

Arnold, Dennis, and Nigel Fortune, eds. *The Beethoven Reader.* New York: Norton, 1971.

Bach, Carl Philipp Emanuel. *Versuch über die wahre Art das Clavier zu spielen.* Berlin: In Verlegung des Auctoris, 1753 and 1762. Translated and edited by William Mitchell as *Essay on the True Art of Playing Keyboard Instruments* (New York: Norton, 1949).

Baker, Nancy Kovaleff, and Thomas Christensen, eds. *Aesthetics and the Art of Musical Composition in the German Enlightenment: Selected Writings of Johann Georg Sulzer and Heinrich Christoph Koch.* Cambridge: Cambridge University Press, 1995.

Baldwin, James. "The Creative Process." In *Creative America,* 17–21. New York: Ridge, 1962.

Beck, Dagmar, and Grita Herre. "Anton Schindlers 'Nutzanwendung' der Cramer-Etüden." In *Zu Beethoven 3,* edited by Harry Goldschmidt, 177–208. Berlin: Verlag Neuer Musik, 1988.

Beethoven, Ludwig van. *Autograph Miscellany from circa 1786 to 1799: British Museum Additional Manuscript 29801, ff. 39–162 (The Kafka Sketchbook).* Edited by Joseph Kerman. 2 vols. London: British Museum, 1970.

———. *Briefwechsel Gesamtausgabe.* Edited by Sieghard Brandenburg. 7 Vols. Munich: G. Henle Verlag, 1996–98.

———. *Keßlersches Skizzenbuch.* Transcribed and edited by Sieghard Brandenburg. 2 vols. Bonn: Beethoven-Haus, 1976, 1978.

———. *Konversationshefte.* Edited by Dagmar Beck and Günther Brosche. Vol. 10. Leipzig: Deutscher Verlag für Musik, 1993.

———. *The Letters of Beethoven.* Translated and edited by Emily Anderson. 3 vols. London: Macmillan, 1961.

———. *Supplemente zur Gesamtausgabe.* Edited by Willy Hess. Vol. 9. Wiesbaden: Breitkopf und Härtel, 1959.

Bekker, Paul. *The Orchestra*. New York: Norton, 1936.

Bion. "The Lament for Adonis." In *Theocritus, Bion, and Moschus Rendered into English Prose,* edited and translated by Andrew Lang, 172–73. London: Macmillan, 1901.

Bloom, Harold. *The Anxiety of Influence: A Theory of Poetry*. New York: Oxford University Press, 1973; 2d ed., 1997.

Brandenburg, Sieghard, ed. *Beethoven, Werke für Klavier und Violine*. Vol. 1. Munich: Henle, 1974.

———. "Bemerkungen zu Beethovens Op. 96." *Beethoven Jahrbuch* 9 (1973–77): 11–25.

———. "Violin Sonatas, Cello Sonatas, and Variations." In *Ludwig van Beethoven,* edited by Joseph Schmidt-Görg and Hans Schmidt, 135–56. New York: Praeger, 1970.

———. "Zur Textgeschichte von Beethovens Violinsonate, op. 47." In *Musik, Edition, Interpretation: Gedenkschrift Günter Henle,* edited by Martin Bente, 111–24. Munich: Henle, 1980.

Breuning, Gerhard von. *Aus dem Schwarzspanierhause: Erinnerungen an Ludwig van Beethoven aus meiner Jugendzeit*. Vienna, 1874. Reprint, Hildesheim: Georg Olms, 1970.

Cahn, Peter. "Aspekte der Schlussgestaltung in Beethovens Instrumentalwerken." *Archiv für Musikwissenschaft* 39, no. 1 (1982): 19–31.

Chew, Geoffrey. "The Christmas Pastorella in Austria, Bohemia, and Moravia." Ph.D. diss., University of Manchester, 1968.

———. "Pastorale." In *The New Grove Dictionary of Music and Musicians,* ed. Stanley Sadie, vol. 14, pp. 290–95. London: Macmillan, 1980.

Cobbett, Walter Wilson, comp. and ed. *Cobbett's Cyclopedic Survey of Chamber Music*. 2d edition, revised by C. Mason. 3 vols. London: Oxford University Press, 1963.

Cooke, Deryck, ed. *Rudolph Réti's Thematic Patterns in Sonatas of Beethoven*. London: Faber and Faber, 1967.

Couperin, François. *L'Art de toucher le clavecin*. Rev ed. Paris: Boivin, 1717 [1716].

———. *L'Art de toucher le clavecin*. Edited by Anna Linde. Wiesbaden: Breitkopf und Härtel, 1961 [1933].

Cramer, Johann Baptist. *21 Etüden für Klavier: Nach dem Handexemplar Beethovens aus dem Besitz Anton Schindlers*. Edited by Hans Kann. Vienna: Universal, 1974.

Curtius, Ernst Robert. *European Literature and the Latin Middle Ages*. Translated by Willard R. Trask. Princeton, N.J.: Princeton University Press, 1953.

Czerny, Carl. *Vollständige theoretische-practische Pianoforteschule, op. 500*. Vienna: Diabelli, 1839.

D'Indy, Vincent. *Beethoven: A Critical Biography*. Translated by Theodore Baker. Boston: Boston Music, 1912.

Dornel, Charles. *Pièces de clavecin*. N.p., 1731.

Drabkin, William. "Towards the 'Symphonic Concerto' of the Middle Period: Beethoven's Third and Fourth Piano Concertos." In *Ludwig van Beethoven: Atti del Convegno Internazionale di Studi, 30 settembre–1 octobre 1988,* edited by Giuseppe Pugliese, 93–103. Treviso, Italy: Matteo editore, 1989.

Drake, Kenneth. *The Sonatas of Beethoven as He Played and Taught Them*. Bloomington: Indiana University Press, 1972.

Edwards, F. G. "George P. Bridgetower and the Kreutzer Sonata." *Musical Times* 49 (1908): 302.

Eibner, Franz. "Einige Kriterien für die Apperzeption und Interpretation von Beethovens Werk." In *Beiträge '76–'78; Beethoven-Kolloquium 1977*. Kassel: Bärenreiter, 1978.

Empson, William. *Some Versions of Pastoral.* London, 1935. Reprint, Norfolk, Conn.: New Directions, 1960.

Engel, Johann Jakob. *Über die musikalische Malerey. In J. J. Engel's Schriften: Reden and asthetische Versuche,* vol. 4. Berlin: Mylius, 1844.

Ettin, Andrew V. *Literature and the Pastoral.* New Haven, Conn.: Yale University Press, 1984.

Fétis, François-Joseph, and Ignaz Moscheles. *Méthode des méthodes.* Paris: M. Schlesinger, 1840. Reprint, Geneva: Minkoff, 1973.

Fishman, Natan. *Kniga eskizov Beethoven za 1802–1803 gody.* 3 vols. Moscow: Gos. Muzykal'noe izd-vo, 1962.

Frimmel, Theodor von. *Beethoven-Studien,* 2 vols. Munich: Müller, 1905, 1906.

Gardeton, César. *Almanach de la musique pour l'an 1819.* Paris, 1820.

Grove, George, ed. *A Dictionary of Music and Musicians.* London: Macmillian, 1879–89.

Hanslick, Eduard. *On the Musically Beautiful: A Contribution Towards the Revision of the Aesthetics of Music.* Translated by Geoffrey Payzant. Indianapolis: Hackett, 1986.

Herwegh, Marcel. *Technique d'interprétation sous forme d'essai d'analyse psychologique expérimental appliquée aux sonates pour piano et violon de Beethoven.* Paris: Magasin Musical, 1926.

Hess, Willy, ed. *Verzeichnis der nicht in der Gesamtausgabe veröffentlichten Werke Ludwig van Beethovens.* No. 46. Wiesbaden: Breitkopf und Härtel, 1957.

Horton, John. *Mendelssohn Chamber Music.* London: British Broadcasting Corporation, 1972.

Hummel, Johann Nepomuk. *A Complete Theoretical and Practical Course of Instructions, on the Art of Playing the Piano Forte.* London: T. Boosey, 1827?–28.

Jander, Owen. "The 'Kreutzer' Sonata as Dialogue." *Early Music* 16 (1988): 34–49.

Jauss, Hans Robert. *Toward an Aesthetic of Reception.* Translated by Timothy Bahti. Minneapolis: University of Minnesota Press, 1982.

Johnson, Douglas P. *Beethoven's Early Sketches in the "Fischhof Miscellany."* Ann Arbor: UMI, 1980.

Johnson, Douglas, Alan Tyson, and Robert Winter. *The Beethoven Sketchbooks: History, Reconstruction, Inventory.* Berkeley: University of California Press, 1985.

Jonas, Oswald. "Beethovens Skizzen und ihre Gestaltung zum Werk." *Zeitschrift für Musikwissenschaft* 16 (1934): 456–59.

Kahl, Willi. "Zu Beethovens Naturauffassung." In *Beethoven und die Gegenwart: Festschrift Ludwig Schiedermair,* edited by Arnold Schmitz, 220–65. Berlin: F. Dümmlers Verlag, 1937.

Kalkbrenner, Friedrich. *Méthode pour apprendre le pianoforte.* Paris: M. Schlesinger, 1830.
———. *A New Method of Studying the Piano-Forte.* London: D'Almain, 1832.

Kermode, Frank. *The Sense of an Ending: Studies in the Theory of Fiction.* London: Oxford University Press, 1967.

Kinsky, Georg, and Hans Halm. *Das Werk Beethovens.* Munich: Henle, 1955.

Kirkendale, Warren. *Fugue and Fugato in Rococo and Classical Chamber Music.* Translated by Margaret Bent and the author. Durham, N.C.: Duke University Press, 1979.

Knecht, Justin Heinrich. *Vollständige Orgelschule.* Leipzig: Breitkopf, 1795. Reprint, Weisbaden: Breitkopf und Härtel, 1989.

Koch, Heinrich Christoph. *Musikalisches Lexicon.* Frankfurt, 1802. Reprint, Hildesheim: G. Olms, 1964.

Kramer, Richard. "Counterpoint and Syntax: On a Difficult Passage in the First Movement of Beethoven's String Quartet in C minor, Opus 18 No. 4." In *Beiträge zu
Beethovens Kammermusik: Symposion Bonn 1984,* edited by Sieghard Brandenburg
and Helmut Loos, 111–24. Munich: Henle, 1987.

———, ed. *Ludwig van Beethoven: A Sketchbook from the Summer of 1800.* 2 vols. Bonn:
Beethoven-Haus, 1996.

———. *Ludwig van Beethoven: Ein neuentdecktes Skizzenblatt vom Sommer 1800 zu
Beethovens Streichquartett op. 18 Nr. 2, Faksimile der Handschrift mit Übertragung und
Kommentar von Richard Kramer.* Bonn: Beethoven-Haus, 1999.

———. "On the Dating of Two Aspects in Beethoven's Notation for Piano" In *Beethoven-Kolloquium 1977,* edited by Rudolf Klein, 160–73. Kassel, Germany: Bärenreiter,
1978.

Kroll, Mark. "La Belle Exécution." In *Historical Musicology: Sources, Methods, Interpretations,* edited by Stephen Crist and Roberta Marvin. Rochester, N.Y.: University of
Rochester Press, forthcoming.

Krummacher, Friedhelm. *Mendelssohn—der Komponist: Studien zur Kammermusik für
Streicher.* Munich: Wilhelm Fink, 1978.

Kuethen, Hans-Werner. *Kritische Bericht,* pt. 3, vol. 2, for the Piano Concerto No. 3 in
C minor, Opus 37. *Beethoven Werke.* Munich: Henle, 1984.

Kunold, Wulf. *Felix Mendelssohn-Bartholdy und seine Zeit.* Laaber: Laaber-Verlag, 1984.

Kunze, Stefan. *Beethoven: Die Werke im Spiegel seiner Zeit: Gesammelte Konzertberichte und
Rezensionen bis 1830.* Laaber: Laaber-Verlag, 1987.

Le Huray, Peter, and James Day, eds. *Music and Aesthetics in the Eighteenth and Early-
Nineteenth Centuries.* Cambridge: Cambridge University Press, 1981.

Lenz, Wilhelm von. *Beethoven: Eine Kunst-Studie: Kritischer Katalog sämmtlicher Werke
Ludwig van Beethovens mit Analysen derselben.* 4 vols. Hamburg: Hoffmann und
Campe, 1860.

Leux, Irmgard. *Christian Gottlob Neefe (1748–1798).* Leipzig: Fr. Kistner & C. F. W. Siegel,
1925.

Levin, Robert. *Who Wrote the Mozart Four-Wind Concertante?* Stuyvesant, N.Y.: Pendragon, 1988.

Lockwood, Lewis. "Beethoven before 1800: The Mozart Legacy." *Beethoven Forum* 3
(1994): 39–52.

———. "Beethoven's Earliest Sketches for the Eroica Symphony." In *Beethoven: Studies
in the Creative Process,* 134–50. Cambridge, Mass.: Harvard University Press, 1992.

———. "Reshaping the Genre: Beethoven's Piano Sonatas from Op. 22 to Op. 28 (1799–
1801)." *Israel Studies in Musicology* 6 (1996): 1–16.

Löhlein, George Simon. *Clavier-Schule.* Leipzig: Waisenhaus und Fromman, 1765.

Maffei, Scipione. "Nuova invenzione d'un gravicembalo col piano e forte." *Giornale
de'letterati d'Italia* (Venice) 5 (1711): 144–59.

Matthews, Denis. *Beethoven.* Master Musicians Series. New York: Vintage, 1988.

Mies, Paul. *Beethoven's Sketches: An Analysis of His Style Based on a Study of His Sketchbooks.* Translated by Doris L. Mackinnon. Oxford, 1929. Reprint, New York: Dover
Books, 1974.

Mikulicz, Karl Lothar. *Ein Notierungsbuch von Beethoven.* Leipzig, 1927. Reprint, Hildesheim: G. Olms, 1972.

Milchmeyer, Johann Peter. *Die wahre Art das Pianoforte zu Spielen.* Dresden: C. C. Mein-
hold, 1797.

Newman, William S. *Beethoven on Beethoven.* New York: Norton, 1988.

———. *The British Encyclopaedia.* London, 1809.

———. "Concerning the Accompanied Clavier Sonata." *Musical Quarterly* 33 (1947):
327–49.

———. *The Sonata in the Classic Era.* New York: Norton, 1983.

Nivers, Guillaume. *Premier livre d'orgue.* Paris, 1665.

Nottebohm, Gustav. *Beethoveniana: Aufsätze und Mittheilungen.* Leipzig: C. F. Peters,
1872. Reprinted as *Beethoveniana von Gustav Nottebohm.* New York: Johnson Reprints, 1970.

———. *Zweite Beethoveniana: Nachgelassene Aufsätze.* 2 vols. Leipzig: C. F. Peters, 1887;
repr., New York: Johnson Reprints, 1970.

Obelkevich, Mary Rowen. "The Growth of a Musical Idea—Beethoven's Opus 96."
Current Musicology 11 (1971): 91–114.

Palisca, Claude, ed. *Norton Anthology of Western Music.* 2 vols. New York: Norton,
1980.

Pauer, Ernst. *The Art of Pianoforte Playing.* London: Novello, 1877.

Peters, Frank. "The Phantom Supercollector of Buried Treasures." *St. Louis Post-Dispatch,* 21 January 1973, p. 5C.

Plantinga, Leon. "When Did Beethoven Compose His Third Piano Concerto?" *Journal
of Musicology* 7 (1989): 275–307.

Poggioli, Renato. *The Oaten Flute: Essays on Pastoral Poetry and the Pastoral Ideal.* Cambridge, Mass.: Harvard University Press, 1975.

Raison, André. *Livre d'orgue.* Paris, 1688.

Rameau, J. P. *Pièces de clavessin.* Paris: Boivin, Hocherau, 1724.

Ratner, Leonard. *Classic Music: Expression, Form, and Style.* New York: Schirmer Books,
1980.

Reeser, Eduard, ed. *Wolfgang Amadeus Mozart: Neue Ausgabe sämtliche Werke.* Vol. 23/
2. Kassel, Germany: Bärenreiter, 1965.

Reynolds, Christopher. "Ends and Means in the Second Finale to Beethoven's Op. 30,
no. 1." In *Beethoven Essays: Studies in Honor of Elliot Forbes,* edited by Lewis Lockwood
and Phyllis Benjamin, 127–45. Cambridge, Mass.: Harvard University Dept. of
Music, 1984.

Richter, Arnd. *Mendelssohn: Leben, Werke, Dokumente.* Mainz and Munich: Piper/Schott,
1994.

Riezler, Walter. *Beethoven.* Translated by George Douglas Henzell Pidcock. London:
Forrester, 1938.

Roeder, Michael Thomas. *A History of the Concerto.* Portland, Ore.: Amadeus, 1994.

Rosen, Charles. *The Classical Style: Haydn, Mozart, Beethoven.* New York: Viking, 1971.

Rosenblum, Sandra P. *Performance Practices in Classic Piano Music.* Bloomington: Indiana University Press, 1988.

Rostal, Max. *Beethoven, the Sonatas for Piano and Violin: Thoughts on Their Interpretation.*
London: Toccata, 1985.

Rousseau, Jean-Jacques. *Dictionnaire de musique.* Paris, 1768. Reprint, Geneva: Minkoff,
1998.

Rowland, David. *A History of Pianoforte Pedalling.* Cambridge: Cambridge University Press, 1993.

Rücker, Andreas. "Beethovens Klaviersatz—Technik und Stilistik." Ph.D. diss., Heidelberg University, 1999.

Sadie, Stanley, ed. *New Grove Dictionary of Music and Musicians.* London: Macmillan, 1980.

Saint-Lambert, M. de. *Principes du clavecin.* Paris: Christophe Ballard, 1702. Translated and edited by Rebecca Harris-Warrick as *Principles of the Harpsichord.* Cambridge: Cambridge University Press, 1984.

Sandberger, Adolf. *Ausgewählte Aufsätze zur Musikgeschichte.* 2 vols. 2. Munich: Drei Masken, 1921, 1924.

Schachter, Carl. "The Sketches for the Sonata for Piano and Violin, Op. 24." *Beethoven Forum* 3 (1994): 107–25.

Schenker, Heinrich. *The Art of Performance.* Translated by Irene Schreier. Edited by Heribert Esser. New York: Oxford University Press, 2000.

Scherman, Thomas K., and Louis Biancolli, eds. *The Beethoven Companion.* Garden City, N.Y.: Doubleday, 1972.

Schiedermair, Ludwig. *Der junge Beethoven.* Leipzig: Quelle und Meyer, 1925.

Schindler, Anton F. *Biographie von Ludwig van Beethoven.* 2d ed. Münster: Aschendorff, 1840. Third edition translated by Constance Jolly as *Beethoven as I Knew Him,* edited by Donald W. MacArdle (Chapel Hill: University of North Carolina Press, 1966).

Schmidt, Hans. "Die Beethovenhandschriften des Beethovenhauses in Bonn." *Beethoven Jahrbuch* 7 (1969–70): 229–30.

Scholem, Gershom, and Theodor W. Adorno. *The Correspondence of Walter Benjamin, 1910–1940.* Translated by Manfred R. Jacobson and Evelyn M. Jacobson. Chicago: University of Chicago Press, 1994.

Schwarz, Boris. "Beethoven and the French Violin School." *Musical Quarterly* 43 (1958): 431–47.

———. Review of *Kniga eskizov Beethoven za 1802–1803 gody,* by Natan Fishman. *Musical Quarterly* 49 (1963): 525.

Skowroneck, Tilman. "Keyboard Instruments of the Young Beethoven." In *Beethoven and His World,* ed. Scott Burnham and Michael Steinberg, 151–92. Princeton, N.J.: Princeton University Press, 2000.

Staehelin, Martin. *Hans Georg Nägeli and Ludwig van Beethoven.* Zurich: Hug, 1982.

Stephan, Rudolf. "Über Mendelssohns Kontrapunkt: Vorläufige Bemerkungen." In *Das Problem Mendelssohn,* edited by Carl Dahlhaus, 201–7. Regensburg, Germany: Gustav Bosse, 1974.

Thayer, Alexander Wheelock. *Ludwig van Beethoven's Leben.* Translated by Hermann Deiters. Vol. 2. Berlin: W. Weber, 1872.

———. *Ludwig van Beethovens Leben.* Edited by Hugo Riemann from the revised edition by Hermann Deiters (1901). 5 vols. Leipzig: Breitkopf und Härtel, 1907–17.

———. *Thayer's Life of Beethoven.* Revised and edited by Elliot Forbes. Princeton, N.J.: Princeton University Press, 1964, 1967.

Tolstoy, Leo. *The Kreutzer Sonata.* Translated by Louise and Aylmer Maude and J. D. Duff. Oxford: Oxford University Press, 1997 [1890].

Tovey, Donald Francis. *Essays in Musical Analysis.* 6 vols. London: Oxford University Press, 1935–39.

———. *Essays in Musical Analysis: Chamber Music.* Edited by Hubert J. Foss. London: Oxford University Press, 1944.

Türk, Daniel Gottlob. *Klavierschule, oder Anweisung zum Klavierspielen für Lehrer und Lernende.* Leipzig and Halle: Schwickert, Hemmerde, und Schwetschke, 1789, 1802.

Tyson, Alan. "The 1803 Version of Beethoven's *Christus am Oelberge.*" *Musical Quarterly* 67 (1970): 551–84. Reprinted in *The Creative World of Beethoven,* edited by P. H. Lang, 49–82. New York: Norton, 1971.

———. "Notes on Five of Beethoven's Copyists." *Journal of the American Musicological Society* 22 (1970): 439–71.

———. "The 'Razumovsky' Quartets: Some Aspects of the Sources." In *Beethoven Studies 3,* ed. Tyson, 107–40. Cambridge: Cambridge University Press, 1982.

Wackenroder, Wilhelm Heinrich. *Phantasien über die Kunst für Freunde der Kunst* (Hamburg, 1799). English-langage translation, *Confessions and Fantasies.* Edited by Mary Hurst Schubert. University Park: Pennsylvania State University Press, 1971.

Wagner, Hans, ed. *Wien von Maria Theresia bis zur Franzosenzeit: Aus den Tagebüchern des Grafen Karl von Zinzendorf.* Vienna: Wiener Bibliophile Gesellschaft, 1972.

Wallace, Robin. *Beethoven's Critics.* Cambridge: Cambridge University Press, 1986.

Weber, Gottfried. *Versuch einer geordneten Theorie der Tonsetzkunst zum Selbstunterricht.* Vol. 2. Mainz: B. Schott, 1818.

Wegeler, Franz Gerhard, and Ferdinand Ries. *Biographische Notizen über Beethoven.* Coblenz: K. Bädeker, 1838. Translated by Frederick Noonan as *Beethoven Remembered: The Biographical Notes of Franz Wegeler and Ferdinand Ries* (Arlington, Va.: Great Ocean, 1987).

Werner, Eric. *Mendelssohn: A New Image of the Composer and His Age.* Translated by Dika Newlin. New York: Free Press of Glencoe, 1963.

Wetzel, Justus Hermann. *Beethovens Violinsonaten.* Vol 1. (no further volumes). Berlin: Max Hesse, 1924.

Wieck, Friedrich. *Piano and Song.* Edited by Nancy Reich. New York: Da Capo, 1982.

Wolff, Christoph, ed. *The String Quartets of Haydn, Mozart, and Beethoven: Studies of the Autograph Manuscripts.* Cambridge, Mass.: Harvard University Dept. of Music, 1980.

Zimmerman, Pierre-Joseph-Guillman. *Encyclopédie du Pianiste—Compositeur.* Paris: L'Auteur, 1840.

Contributors

SUHHNE AHN serves on the faculty and administration of Peabody Conservatory of Music in Baltimore. She did her undergraduate work at Yale and her graduate work in musicology at Harvard. Her doctoral dissertation was entitled "Genre, Style, and Compositional Procedure in Beethoven's 'Kreutzer' Sonata, Opus 47" (1997).

SIEGHARD BRANDENBURG is the former director of the Beethoven-Archiv in Bonn. Among his many contributions to Beethoven scholarship is his work as editor-in-chief of the first critical edition of the Beethoven letters, published by Henle Verlag, Munich. His other publications include many articles and his critical editions of the "Kessler" sketchbook (Munich, 1976) and of the Beethoven Violin Sonatas for the current Beethoven *Werke*. He issued an annotated facsimile edition of the autograph manuscript of the "Pastoral" Symphony.

WILLIAM DRABKIN is a reader in music at the University of Southampton, England. His Ph.D dissertation (Princeton, 1978) deals with the compositional genesis of Beethoven's Piano Sonata in C Minor, Opus 111, and his other publications include articles on Beethoven, analysis, and classical chamber music. He is the general editor of the translation of Heinrich Schenker's *Masterwork in Music* and other translations of Schenker's writings. He recently published *A Reader's Guide to Haydn's Early String Quartets* (Westport, Conn., 2000).

LEWIS LOCKWOOD is the Fanny Peabody Research Professor of Music at Harvard University. His fields of study in music have centered mainly on the Italian Renaissance and Beethoven. His publications, in addition to many articles, include *Beethoven: Studies in the Creative Process* (Cambridge, 1992) and *Beethoven: The Music and the Life* (New York, 2002). He received the Einstein and Kinkeldey Awards of the American Musicological Society and is an honorary member of that society, as well as being a scholarly adviser to the Beethoven-Archiv in Bonn.

RICHARD KRAMER is a Distinguished Professor of Music at the CUNY Graduate Center in New York. He received his Ph.D from Princeton University in 1974 with a dissertation on the sketches for Beethoven's Violin Sonatas Opus 30 and has since published much other Beethoven scholarship, including his edition of *A Sketchbook from the Summer of 1800* (Bonn, 1996). His book *Distant Cycles: Schubert and the Conceiving of Song* was published in 1994.

MARK KROLL is one of the world's leading harpsichordists and fortepianists. He has won critical acclaim for his virtuosity and expressive concert performances and for his numerous recordings. He has appeared as concerto soloist with the world's leading orchestras and is presently harpsichordist for the Boston Symphony Orchestra. Kroll's publications include two editions of Johann Nepomuk Hummel's arrangements of works by Mozart, Beethoven, and others; articles on Hummel's music treatise and those of other writers; and essays on performance practices for the harpsichord and early piano. He has been a guest professor in Germany, Italy, and Yugoslavia and is professor emeritus at Boston University, where he served for many years as chairman of the Department of Historical Performance.

MAYNARD SOLOMON is the author or editor of four books on Beethoven, including his well-known *Beethoven* (New York, 1977; rev. ed., 1998), which has been translated into eight languages. He is a three-time winner of the ASCAP–Deems Taylor Award and his *Beethoven Essays* won the Kinkeldey Award of the American Musicological Society for the most distinguished book in the field published in the year 1989. He has taught at CUNY Graduate Center, the State University of New York at Stony Brook, Columbia, Yale, and Harvard. He is a scholarly adviser to the Beethoven-Archiv in Bonn, Fellow of the New York University Institute for the Humanities, and presently a faculty member at the Juilliard School of Music.

Index

The University of Illinois Press
is a founding member of the
Association of American University Presses.

———————————————————

Composed in 9.5/13 ITC Stone Serif
with Avalon display
by Jim Proefrock
at the University of Illinois Press
Designed by Paula Newcomb
Manufactured by Sheridan Books, Inc.

University of Illinois Press
1325 South Oak Street
Champaign, IL 61820-6903
www.press.uillinois.edu